Doing the Right Thing

Doing the Right Thing

The Importance of Wellbeing in the Workplace

Theo Theobald
&
Cary Cooper

Pro Vice Chancellor (External Relations) and
Professor of Organizational Psychology and Health, Lancaster University

palgrave
macmillan

First published 2012 by
PALGRAVE MACMILLAN

Palgrave Macmillan in the UK is an imprint of Macmillan Publishers Limited, registered in England, company number 785998, of Houndmills, Basingstoke, Hampshire RG21 6XS.

Palgrave Macmillan in the US is a division of St Martin's Press LLC, 175 Fifth Avenue, New York, NY 10010.

Palgrave Macmillan is the global academic imprint of the above companies and has companies and representatives throughout the world.

Palgrave® and Macmillan® are registered trademarks in the United States, the United Kingdom, Europe and other countries

ISBN-13: 978-0-230-29844-6

This book is printed on paper suitable for recycling and made from fully managed and sustained forest sources. Logging, pulping and manufacturing processes are expected to conform to the environmental regulations of the country of origin.

A catalogue record for this book is available from the British Library.

A catalogue record for this book is available from the Library of Congress.

10 9 8 7 6 5 4 3 2 1
21 20 19 18 17 16 15 14 13 12

Printed and bound in Great Britain by
MPG Group, Bodmin and King's Lynn

CONTENTS

What would Mum do?

For openers, it's the kind of question we would probably prefer not to ask ourselves in the workplace too often.

Not when she brought us up to be compassionate and caring, to think about others, to help out and be modest about it, to not tell lies or cheat or be unkind. Put simply, she encouraged us 'to do the right thing'.

But Mum, for all her virtues, wouldn't really understand the stresses of today's workplace, the demands upon us, the expectation we'll perform for longer hours each passing year. Mum wouldn't know the feeling of being passed over for promotion, discriminated against because we stood for what we believed in or challenged for speaking our minds.

This is part of the dichotomy of modern working life. We know what is 'right', but we need to survive, maybe even to thrive if we are to be recognised as a success by our partners, our peers, perhaps even the neighbours.

If you've cracked it, if you're already doing the right thing in the workplace, you should be congratulated, it's difficult. If not, which is most of us, you may not like everything you read here. But this book is not your conscience, it's just a reminder that you may have once had better intentions, that some of your idealism has been eroded over time and it's not too late to reclaim some of that ground.

The reality of the modern world of work includes some unpalatable facts about the way we operate, some bullying regimes, some lazy colleagues, some malpractice which, if not actually criminal, may still be immoral. And it is these home truths which might be tough to face up to.

Recent commercial history is littered with tales of badly run organisations, sometimes where the entire enterprise has been built on sand, only shored up by the duplicity of its senior managers. Finance houses across the globe have been culpable in trading practice that many of us question the ethics of. Fair trade is still a marginal activity, with exploitation happening in one part of the world, so consumers can benefit from lower prices in another.

But hold on, it's not all doom and gloom, there are many examples of good practice, of ethical trading from organisations which clearly value their people and the wider world they operate within. Far from being pessimistic over the future of the workplace, we believe in the essential goodness of most people. The difficulty is in remembering how to behave in a way which we know is right, in order to keep ourselves on the straight and narrow, and foster a working environment where staff are less stressed and more prepared to give of their best. This is not at odds with a profit ethic, as we shall go on to discuss in detail later.

We haven't set out to be deliberately provocative, but while researching and writing this book we came across people who told us stories about the places they worked, and how 'the right thing' was a rarity, a thing of the past. These candid confessions are not likely to endear them to others in their profession, so we have promised confidentiality. Otherwise, how would we ever get to the truth, how would we know what was wrong, how would we be able to implement 'the right thing'?

Equally, we are aware there is much discussion and debate about this topic at present. Some have dismissed the 'happiness agenda' as 'fluffy', an attempt to make us feel good in bad times. But the weight of evidence is too strong to deny the tangible benefits for organisations and individuals.

Our take on the subject is an attempt to present and examine the evidence, to find practical ways of implementing the recommendations and to make wellbeing a significant consideration in our everyday lives. We all owe it to ourselves.

And if the popular drive for happiness is replaced by a new fad next year, we hope to prove personal wellbeing is here to stay for anyone who desires a 'life well lived'.

Acknowledgements

The authors wish to acknowledge the work of the Foresight Project on behalf of the Government Office for Science, published in the work 'Mental Capital and Wellbeing', and of the New Economics Foundation in further developing the five steps to wellbeing.

In addition, we recognise the excellent work of the Chartered Institute of Personnel and Development and many other agencies who actively promote good wellbeing in the workplace.

And finally we applaud the efforts of the many thousands of managers who approach their roles with compassion, empathy and understanding. Managers who strive to do 'the right thing' every day of their working lives.

INTRODUCTION

We recognise wellbeing is a hot topic in the workplace right now, which is why the timing of this book is important. Equally, we all know trends in business come and go, and so need to ensure this does not become simply another 'flavour of the month' The wellbeing of our staff and ourselves is too important for that.

If we had not already begun to embrace the causes, benefits and constructs of wellbeing, global economic conditions in recent times would inevitably have forced it upon us. Organisations are shrinking, competition is increasing, the need to do more, with less resource, is commonplace, and the continual threat of redundancy for many ratchets up the pressure.

Large organisations have appointed a 'head of wellbeing' to make everything better, many SME's meanwhile cross their fingers and hope individuals will be sensible about their health. Indeed, an entire industry of 'wellness' has emerged from nowhere, including companies offering online diagnostics, the appearance of 'wellbeing coaches and consultants' and a plethora of articles, books and studies on the subject.

And it is because of all the 'noise' surrounding the topic, we have attempted to take a more measured view of what is happening. The Foresight project (Cooper et al 2009) is a major, government sponsored study into the subject of the wellbeing of a nation. One of most significant sections of the study covered the world of work, and the effects of many factors on the mental capital within our organisations. The significant conclusions from this study form the foundations of this book, but there is more as well. You will find a section dedicated to behavioural changes each of us can make, to increase the chances of staying mentally fit. However, we have also tried to set this in the context of the modern workplace, offering some interpretation of these behaviours and looking at their role as part of a complete package, which also contains some thoughts on the work environment, the harmonisation of sometimes disparate parts of our lives and practical strategies to incorporate some different ways of working.

Throughout the text you will find many real life examples, taken from interviews with workers and managers at different stages in their careers. Although not formal case studies, these real people illustrate a wide range of the problems and solutions many of us face in the workplace. There are working parents, desperately attempting to balance the significant roles they play; stressed and stuck middle managers caught between unfulfilling work and the threat of redundancy; and weary workaholics who have no idea how to switch off the treadmill. These 'types' are not uncommon in today's world of work, in fact we may see some of ourselves in them, but help is at hand.

We begin with an examination of happiness and wellbeing. Logic dictates that as individuals we want to live the 'best' life we can, though we could argue about that word for another thousand pages! If we agree wellbeing and happiness are a major part of this ambition, a good starting point is the consideration of each of these terms, and the relationship we have with them in the world of work.

It is a short leap from the workplace to home life (all too short for some!), so we will inevitably talk about the effects of increased wellbeing in our personal lives too. However, our main ambition is to set the subject in a work context for a couple of reasons. Firstly, work now forms such a large part of many of our lives, we cannot hope to 'live better' if we don't get things right from 9 to 5, (substitute your own ridiculous working hours here if you wish). Secondly, for many of us, we have a sphere of influence in the workplace. This might be a formalised structure where we are managing other people, or we may simply have relationships with peers. Either way, we have the ability to affect their wellbeing. There is a strong moral case for wanting to do this, some might think of it as 'societal duty', we simply call it 'the right thing'.

An inevitable and well documented malaise of the modern workplace is stress, so we will move on to outline why this is happening and increasing year on year. In many senses this is at the core of the issue we seek to solve, as stress reduction has a direct correlation with better wellbeing.

A greater understanding of how we got to where we are, will help us to consider some antidotes, so today's major workplace issues are identified and examined in detail. From here we have a platform of knowledge to begin building strategies into our everyday lives, which will attempt to overcome some of the toxicity of the modern workplace.

We think it is likely that some of our recommendations will already be part of your everyday routine, but it is the combination of all of them, on a regular basis, which will begin to make a difference. This rationale is important in giving us both justification and incentive to change the way we work. The actions we outline are also underpinned, in many cases, by scientific evidence.

Finally, this is not some hare-brained, self-help programme with promises to bring you success beyond compare, rather it is a considered, realistic and sustainable set of behavioural changes, which you have the option of adopting if you so choose. The benefits will be realised in the longer term, if the recommendations are exercised consistently, and their efficacy is backed by some of the most up to date and rigorous research into work-based issues which is currently available.

CHAPTER 1

Setting the context of wellbeing at work

Defining the right thing

It is difficult to argue in favour of the right thing, without coming across as prissy and moralising, but that is not the intention. Instead what we are trying to do is prove a case for managing ourselves, our operations and our people, in a way which has the best outcome for all concerned.

The tricky part comes when you attempt to unpick this and establish exactly what 'best' means to all the parties involved. In global terms, 'best' might mean eradicating poverty and stopping all wars; that would surely be the right thing. But we don't seem to have proven ourselves very good at this. As comedian Marcus Brigstocke says, 'if everyone who claimed they wanted world peace really meant it, then we'd have it'.

In a commercial environment, 'best' might mean greatest profit, most sustainable trading, happiest workforce or any number of other objectives. This is where the essential conundrum of 'the right thing' first emerges. One of the main barriers to achieving it, is that on first examination, pursuing a course of action which is beneficial in one regard (say profit), might be directly at odds with what is 'right' in another area (say employee wellbeing). Is child labour justifiable so we can buy cheaper clothes? The moral answer must be 'no', yet it still happens.

Our assertion is that 'best' can only be delivered across the board if a long term view is taken of 'the right thing' making the outputs deliverable and sustainable over time, with profits gained against a backdrop of sound moral principles. All this might sound a bit high and mighty, but by using reasoned argument to support our case and practical work-based experience to keep the theories well grounded, we hope very much to avoid any accusation of sanctimony.

For many years, economists and psychologists have been fascinated by the relationship between output, or productivity and happiness or wellbeing in the workplace. Organisations as diverse as the University of Warwick (Oswald 1997), and the Chartered Institute of Personnel and Development have published papers on the topic. There is growing weight of evidence of a direct linkage, so if it appears at first sight that working the staff harder, and ignoring their environmental and social needs will result in low costs and higher profits, both the science and common sense increasingly suggest this state of affairs is not sustainable.

So let us balance the altruism we might feel with the plain reality that what is good for it's own sake, the behaviours that Mum taught us, is also the right thing for organisations committed to long term success.

Our current happiness

We seem to be surrounded by self-help advice. There are masses of column inches on happiness and wellbeing, but are we really in such a poor state, do we actually need 'fixing' at all?

When we consider the work done by Abraham Maslow, on his hierarchy of needs, we are already sated in many of the areas which form the foundations of our existence. In developed countries, lack of food and shelter has all but been eradicated, our financial wealth has never been greater, and with this comes choice and freedom, important elements in the building of self-worth. What can possibly be wrong with us?

In spite of all the material things we are now able to buy, there is a paradox. What most of us claim to want is a return to simpler times. We may not have been so cash rich back then, but we had meaningful relationships, knew there were people looking out for us. We had time, time to appreciate the wonders of the world around us.

It felt like people were more giving, more sharing; didn't our parents' generation simply worry less? Even without the rose-tinted spectacles, the past looked brighter than the present.

It's certainly true, that in our lifetime we have pursued and in the main won a higher standard of living, but though we thought this would make us more complete, it's done anything but. The words of Oscar Wilde were never truer than applied to today's society, for it seems we know the price of everything and the value of nothing.

Only now, after decades of relentless growth, do we seem ready and anxious, (perhaps because of the more austere times we now live in) to reclaim the 'happiness' which was once within our grasp.

The politics of happiness

It seems even politicians have grasped the most important measurement should be more of an index of life satisfaction, rather than a hard metric of cash-at-bank.

As far back as 1968, Robert Kennedy displayed his visionary genius when he echoed Oscar Wilde's wisdom and declared, 'Gross National Product measures everything except that which makes life worthwhile'. What he realised is the conventional measures we had put in place, might give us a relative view of prosperity year on year, but they signally failed to capture how fulfilled we were.

He summarised it in this way, '...it does not allow for the health of our children, the quality of their education or the joy of their play. It does not include the beauty of our poetry or the strength of our marriages, the intelligence of our public debate or the integrity of our public officials'.

Similarly in Britain, Winston Churchill understood the necessity for a broad view of the nation's worth. An early manifestation of the Arts Council had been set up during the Second World War, so performers and artists could continue their craft, with the intention of keeping spirits and morale high in dark times. When urged to divert funding from these activities into the war effort, Churchill replied, 'Then what are we fighting for?'

A measure for wellbeing

When it comes to measuring wellbeing, a much broader approach is needed and this role has been taken on by, amongst others, a U.K. based organisation called the Legatum Institute (www.prosperity.com), which produces an annual survey and report on a global basis. Much of the output of their study is freely available online. In seeking to uncover some of the qualitative elements which Robert Kennedy spoke of, the Institute goes beyond simply totting up the prosperity of nations in economic terms, it also looks at levels of health and education plus the safety, security and personal freedom which people feel they have.

In full the elements of the Legatum Prosperity Index are listed below:

- Economy
- Entrepreneurship and opportunity
- Governance
- Education
- Health
- Safety and security
- Personal freedom
- Social capital

At the top of the rankings in 2010 were the Scandinavian countries of Norway, Denmark and Finland, the United States came in at number 10, with the U.K. a few places behind at 13. Some of the poorest African nations are at the foot of the table, which shows us that there *can* be a correlation between financial wealth and many of the other measure which might make us happy. It is not the money itself which increases satisfaction, but rather that, at the extremes, the lack of it may lead to higher crime, poorer health care, less developed education systems and reduced personal freedom. It is, in effect, deprivation which can contribute actively and in the longer term to unhappiness.

Some interesting results occur mid-table, where China for example sits at number 58. It's position is bolstered by a strong economy, but the overall score is damaged by low marks for safety, security and personal freedom.

Perhaps the most interesting measure for us to look at is that of social capital, especially with regard to the effect this has on success levels in business. The way social capital is explained, is via a range of measures like 'how charitable people are', 'what level of volunteering goes on', 'the strength of family', 'community ties' and 'the amount of joining in with social, leisure based and civic groups'.

As an employer, we might be forgiven for thinking that this is a 'nice to have', but the effects of social capital go beyond our behaviour in the community, they extend further into the workplace, the Legatum report states, '...societies with lower levels of social capital have been shown to experience lower levels of economic growth'. When people's wellbeing is improved, so their efficiency, productivity or quality of output gets better in line'. The report goes on to state, 'The use of the term "capital" reflects an important reality: social networks are an asset that produces economic and wellbeing returns'.

We continually return to the theme of wellbeing and output, stating that in spite of what many business owners and leaders believe, these two elements are not mutually exclusive. Treating workers better will not damage the bottom line, by contrast, they will contribute more. The work done by Legatum helps to bear this out. Many of us have personal experience of this. Our output increases when we are well looked after.

Measures of happiness (Dolan et al 2011) have certainly become more sophisticated, especially in the U.S., where researchers have attempted to go a step beyond the universally recognised categories used by Legatum and the like. Here, the seemingly simple process of asking people if they're happy has been employed. There is a difficulty to overcome, as often the reply is hard to validate, according to when people are being asked and by whom.

An employee survey may lead staff to declare less happiness than they really feel, in the belief it will keep management on it's toes. However, admitting a lack of happiness to a social peer group (or indeed ourselves) can be seen as an admission of failure, a 'loser' mentality. How then can we make the data more robust?

One way would be to ask what it is that makes people happy; let's say a respondent has said, 'spending time with the family'. It is then possible to measure over a set period of days, how many minutes are spent in this 'activity' and to track this as a measure of happiness.

On days where more time has been spent with the family, the survey subject should, in theory, give a more positive response to the question 'are you happy?'

Paradoxically, it seems that people can be perfectly happy with their lives until you ask them if they are!

Whatever difficulties we might face, we can see that over time the empirical measures are getting more accurate, by employing a range of different tools and techniques, we get to the point where we can start to cross check the story being told (about how happy an individual *says* they are), with what we know to be a suite of objective measures. Taken together the combined data will give a robust result on a 'happiness index'.

In comparison to measures employed in other social sciences, these techniques may still be in their infancy, but the prognosis is good for much more accurate measurement of this 'subjective emotion' in the future. An uplift in the accuracy of data can lead to better happiness tracking, which in turn should help to validate the strategies which work and increase our wellbeing.

Conclusions

Doing the right thing seeks the best outcome for everybody

Nations are waking up to the fact that GDP is a poor measure of wellbeing, we need to think wider

Factors like freedom and social capital (what we do for each other) are becoming more significant

Measurements of wellbeing are becoming more sophisticated all the time

CHAPTER 2

The relationship between happiness and wellbeing

Before we get drawn into a confusion of meanings, we need to consider the difference between happiness and wellbeing. Although the terms are often used in an interchangeable way, there are shades of difference between them. For our purposes, we would view 'wellbeing' as a state of contentment, if it's not too obvious to say it, it is the state of 'being well', which is different from 'being happy'. We think of 'happiness' as being closer to complete fulfilment, something we have all experienced, but by its nature is a transient state. We would go on to argue part of the feeling of being happy is the ability to compare one set of circumstances to another.

This is one reason why nostalgia plays such a large part in happiness. When asked about the happiest times of their lives, many respondents hark back to childhood. This regression is not surprising, as it takes us to a time in our lives when everything was much simpler and we had little responsibility. However, along with the weight on our shoulders of a mortgage, a job to hold down, relationships to juggle, we also get many benefits from being 'grown up'. We get choice (something we didn't always have in childhood), relative wealth (not just pocket money) and the maturity of knowing which behaviours to pursue to make us happy. If you really could measure your childhood happiness, would the index show you as being 'more at one with the world' than you are now, or is it simply the comparison of states which makes us believe we were happier then?

The 'scarcity' of happiness seems also to be a factor. Few report being happy all the time, so when it has happened we tend to cherish the memory of it. Let's say it was a day spent on the beach as a child, with siblings and our parents. Within this scene, there are many elements which could be the source of happiness, family relationships, a beautiful environment, the sun on our faces, ice cream, exercise, we can each make our own list. However it is often the 'differentness' of the occasion which contributes to our happiness. It is the fact of this being a *rare* occasion which increases our love of it, and our desire to treasure the memory. As time passes, the accuracy of that memory may fade, and we begin to imbue it with whatever happiness triggers are in our subconscious. We could call it the 'those were the days' syndrome.

By contrast, 'wellbeing' can be sustained over a longer period of time. It may help to think of it as a maintenance schedule. A set of routines we carry out and a suite of conscious actions we take, in order to keep ourselves well. This is easy to grasp if we are just thinking of our physical wellness. We know diet, fitness and the avoidance of toxins are key elements, but we can apply similar 'treatment' to our emotional wellness too. We will examine this in detail later.

However, it is hard to see how either state could live alone, and it is maybe useful to see wellbeing as a stepping stone on the way to happiness, remove it and the gap cannot be bridged. This is the reason why 'wellbeing at work' is so important in helping people to live fulfilled, complete lives. Spend 8 to 10 hours a day without the stepping stone in place, and it's virtually impossible to garner the confidence to make the leap across the gulf to happiness when you return home.

Combining wellbeing and happiness together, we are simply aiming to define a 'best state' (i.e. some sense of living a 'good life' as seen both by others and critically by ourselves), Sometimes this peer judgement is an element of our mood state, so to be respected, admired or loved by others around us might be the strongest construct of our happiness.

Let us begin to consider what the base elements of happiness are, so we might be better equipped to recognise them in our daily lives.

Happiness is sometimes a combination of art and science. If we think of 'art' as creativity and free thinking, and 'science' in terms of logical thought and reasoned argument, then surely both can play their part. The emotion associated with all things artistic may lift our mood, like when we witness the breathtaking beauty of a sunset. Things which are aesthetically pleasing are often also uplifting. By the same token, science and logic can help to explain other elements of our wellbeing, like the endorphin release after vigorous exercise. Each has a connection to our overall life satisfaction. Science is good for making sense of wellbeing and happiness, when we 'are in a good mood, but don't know why'.

And what about the argument over nature or nurture, where does this fit into to defining how happy we are? Often people who should not be happy by any conventional measure can surprise us with their cheery demeanour. In Western society we often marvel at the smiling faces of African children on our television screens. These are kids who have nothing, who live in poverty, are poorly educated and at risk from all kinds of threats, but still they laugh, joke and beam their smiles at the camera.

It would appear their happiness is inherent, not bound by their circumstance. In fact, they are happy *despite* what surrounds them, not because of it. Contrast this with the consumerist attitude of developed countries, where 'what you have is who you are', and our envy of the ability of other people's contentment is easy to understand, it often feels we are much less happy.

Beyond this, there are those who 'break the mould', by 'learning' to be happy through the process of nurture, the way they live their lives. As President Abraham Lincoln once said, 'it is not the years in your life that matter, but the life in your years!'. It seems logical, particularly when we look at the example of the African children, that circumstance plays some role in our wellbeing, but even more significant is our *attitude* to the immediate environment, which may be said to be partly defined by our genetic heritage.

It is here that many arguments about improving wellbeing and happiness hit the buffers, if we can only be as contented as our genes allow, then what's the point in trying to alter this state? If the limit to how happy we can ever be, is defined by who we are now, then the pursuit of greater happiness is surely futile?

But wait, isn't it the case that achieving 'maximum wellbeing' can only ever be a personal thing, something so unique that we cannot build a scientific scale for it. Let us say for the sake of argument that you and your partner are as happy as you can be (as individuals). Who is to say that their happiness is 'greater' or 'lesser' than yours? Because we are identifying the sensation in a unique way, the calibration of happiness from one person to another cannot be accurately measured. Measuring happiness is easier within ourselves when we compare our current level with the way it once was. In a sense, an objective scale of our personal happiness can only happen in retrospect.

Abraham Maslow talked about 'self actualisation' a sense of being at one, but made no attempt to define what it was for each individual. Maybe in fact, it is the idea that this state is not replicated in any other human being which is so appealing for us, reaching our own personal zenith of contentment puts us in an exclusive club of one.

What does all this amount to? It appears that there is good news and bad news, (so you will feel better or worse according to whether you are a glass-half-full, or glass-half-empty person!). Let's get the bad news out of the way first. It seems that there might be a finite limit on how happy you can become, depending on your genes and the sort of person you are.

Leading psychologist Professor Martin Seligman (Seligman 2000), puts forward the theory that our genetic propensity to happiness, defined as the set point (S), can be added to the conditions of our lives (C), and the voluntary activities we choose

(V), to assess our overall happiness (H). Therefore his formula is as follows:

$$H = S + C + V.$$

Whatever the relative significance of the separate factors may be, we can agree that each plays a part. It is therefore logical that you can only increase your own wellbeing and happiness, and that of the people around you in the workplace, up to a certain point.

Now for the good news; there is increasing scientific evidence (Oswald and Wu 2009), to suggest that happiness is not all about fate. Understand more about the drivers of wellbeing and we can pursue them on our own behalf and for our employees, with a much greater likelihood of a 'life better lived' as the result, if all other factors remain equal.

In addition to this, it seems that 'happiness envy' is a pointless emotion, if anything, it actively robs us of some of our potential to be at one. If we accept that a degree of our happiness is genetic, if you like our *propensity* to be happy, then feeling aggrieved about having less of it than someone else, is as pointless as wishing we were taller. Acceptance of what we are is a starting point from which we can move forward.

If the African children or the receptionist at work display (at least outwardly) a degree of happiness that seems beyond ours, then let's be gracious enough to allow them that, without it blighting our own view of the world.

Eventually we may settle to the fact that we have a current wellbeing level and a propensity for it to go up or down, according to circumstance and behaviour. What 'happiness gurus' fail to point out is the complexity of the issue. It is, as Martin Seligman points out, a matrix of interwoven factors which combine in a unique way to bring about our emotional state.

So, we won't make false promises. What we will endeavour to do is examine the factors which are controllable, while seeking to understand how the interrelationship between these and other wellbeing-triggers works.

Conclusions

Wellbeing and happiness are interlinked, but they are not the same thing

Happiness is often transient, but its fleeting nature can be part of the appeal

We can consciously alter our wellbeing if we go about it in the right way

Genetics play a part in our 'happiness potential' but that's not the whole story

We are each unique, it is likely that our happiness is too

CHAPTER 3

Stress factors at work

What might diminish or damage our wellbeing during the 8 plus hours we spend at work?

Let us look at how stress plays out in the modern workplace, what the implications of this are and how we might go about reducing our own stress level and that of the people who surround us. This is, after all central to the ethos of 'doing the right thing'.

In the past we have thought of stressors as a combination of three things, demand (the work we're asked to do), control (how much influence we have over the task, the deadline etc.), and support (who or what resource may be at our disposal) (Karasek et al 1998). These constructs still hold true, but there is more.

Current thinking suggests that stress is brought about by the interrelationship of the individual and the environment, so it cannot be said that stress exists in either one of these things, but in the *transaction* between them by a series of psychological processes. We can use the process of appraisal as an illustrative example.

A situation becomes stressful for an individual when they make an appraisal of the demand upon them, versus the 'total resource' available, so if asked to complete a large number of tasks (demand) in a limited time (the time can be said to be a resource) and, based on experience or educated guesswork, the work in hand looks to be unachievable, then stress will ensue.

Two levels of appraisal take place. Firstly, the individual makes a judgement over 'what might happen' if the task is not completed. In stress prone situations, this is expressed in negative terms (i.e. something will be lost, some threat will be carried out, or 'harm' will ensue in some form).

This judgement will be related to the expectations in the workplace, if a number of boxes have to be packed in a certain time frame, to meet a pick up deadline, workers will easily see the negative repercussions, in terms of cost and annoyance, if the task is not completed. It is the negative knock-on effect which is at the root of the stress.

The second level of appraisal is to do with an assessment of what can be *done* to remedy the situation, and it is during this phase that workers consider what coping resources might come into play, a judgement of their personal resilience.

Coping strategies can be seen to be far more effective if individuals feel supported, so in this case it may mean the physical drafting in of additional resource, (someone to help with the packing), or it can take the psychological form of knowing that others realise you are doing your best in difficult circumstances. In our private and business lives, we all know the benefit of a supportive word or gesture from a friend or co-worker, and this kind of support is vital if stress is to be contained.

For the sake of balance, we should point out that not all stress is bad, and experiencing the adrenaline rush of having to meet a tight deadline may be a positive motivator for many workers. However, if this situation becomes the norm and one deadline is piled on top of another with no respite between, then the stress can turn toxic.

Modern causes of workplace stress

There are many factors which contribute to stress at work and the root cause is often sited around personal relationships. However to understand what drives the behaviour which leads to a breakdown in the personal bond between people, we have to step back and consider what the central issues are.

1. Security – In a Work Foundation survey (Isles 2005), nearly 40% of respondents said they worked long hours because they were afraid of losing their jobs. This is like the fairytale of chicken-licken, when enough people said that the sky was falling, it gained a level of credence beyond its likelihood of happening. The truth is that evidence suggests periods of tenure have not significantly fallen, in fact fewer workers have been made redundant and turnover of staff has stayed static (DTI 2006; Isles 2005).

Perceptions of security have definitely changed, and this has been due to the ripple effect of reorganisations and their attendant redundancies, meaning that beyond the workers who are actually asked to leave the organisation, the 'redundancy-survivors' suffer nearly as much, by fearing for their own futures.

Philip – redundancy victim

'It was just one round of reorganisation after another. Every time it happened you just kept your head below the parapet and hoped for the best. On more than one occasion I was forced to apply for my own job and went up against my co-workers, some of who were also my friends outside work.

I reckon it was about the sixth round that finally got me. By then I'd lived in an insecure limbo-land for about 4 years, so you won't be surprised to know that I was actually relieved when it happened, at least the waiting was over and I could move on with my career elsewhere'.

2. The intensification of work – It is difficult to draw comparisons with past generations over how *hard* work is today, as against 100 years ago. Digging coal and bashing rivets in unpleasant working conditions and environments, with little in the way of worker's rights was certainly no picnic.

However, today's workplace has it's own intensity, brought about by the increase in competition, partly due to globalisation, added to more sophisticated management measures and techniques, plus the move from physical to mental work associated with a decline in manufacturing (Lundberg and Cooper 2010).

Team working and performance-related reward are commonplace, and while on the surface they might simply look like sensible management interventions, they can have a knock-on effect of increasing stress levels. Although there are clear benefits in organising people in teams, and each worker has the chance to be supported by their colleagues, teamwork 'is also associated with work intensification and more performance control by means of financial incentives all of which lead to a more stressful environment' (Smeaton et al 2007). It may be that workers are anxious not to let their colleagues down, particularly if performance-related pay is linked to team output. Alternatively, they may become stressed if a co-worker isn't pulling his/her weight and they feel powerless to intervene.

The increase in the intensification of work carries with it potential for higher levels of sickness absence, with 57% of respondents ranking it in their top three work-based stressors (CIPD annual survey report on absence management 2006).

3. The emotionalisation of work – because the type of work we do has altered, the skill set associated with it has moved too. Many more workers are now engaged in 'relationship' jobs, where they have to interact much more with their colleagues, clients or customers.

In the case of roles which involve relationships outside the organisation, as in customer service jobs, retail or any business that needs to court clients to secure it's future, stress can result in the pressure of 'keeping up appearances'. This is as the result of a dichotomy between *having* to be nice and *feeling* nice. So, for example, the hard pressed waiter in the busy restaurant is being paid to provide service with a smile, while inside he/she could happily strangle the awkward customer. It is this continual 'acting' role which results in stress.

Increasingly companies talk about 'relationship management' with their customers, and the difficulty here, is that *fake* sincerity is unsustainable, wearing and ultimately stressful. We have all been told to 'have a nice day' by a world-weary shop worker. This kind of customer-service-by-rote just doesn't work for any of the parties to it.

Recognising stress

The difficulty with stress is both understanding *when* it is present and calibrating *how much* of it there is. There is no stress thermo-meter to tell us what an 'ideal' level should be, or whether we are above or below that mark. We can rightly conclude stress is personal, affecting each of us differently. Equally, it may be circumstantial. We all have days when things seem to get on top of us, but at other times we are perfectly able to cope with anything the world throws our way.

It might also be the case that we're good at recognising stress in others, but much less able to do so with ourselves. Sometimes, because stress is a point along a line which also has 'lack of wellbeing', 'emotional difficulty', and even 'mental illness' on it, the stigma associated with any kind of failure to cope is enough to put many in denial. This can be particularly prevalent in men, who, generally speaking are less emotionally intelligent (and in touch with their feelings), than their female counter-parts. It is also found in senior management tiers, where resilience is an expectation and falling prey to stress seen as a sign of weakness. This is both unenlightened and dangerous.

Although there is no machine to measure stress levels, some of the behavioural and physical signs are easy to recognise, and becoming aware of this for ourselves and our co-workers, is the first stage of remedy.

Below are two checklists which outline the behavioural and physical symptoms of stress. You may have seen a number of them at play in your workplace.

Behavioural symptoms

- Constant irritability with people
- Feeling unable to cope

- Lack of interest in life
- Constant, or recurring fear of disease
- A feeling of being a failure
- A feeling of being bad or self-hatred
- Difficulty in making decisions
- A feeling of ugliness
- Loss of interest in other people
- Awareness of suppressed anger
- Inability to show true feelings
- A feeling of being the target of other people's animosity
- Loss of sense of humour
- Feeling of neglect
- Dread of the future
- Feeling of having failed as a person or parent
- A feeling of having no-one to confide in
- Difficulty in concentrating
- Inability to finish one task before rushing to another
- An intense fear of open or enclosed spaces or of being alone

Physical symptoms

- Lack of appetite
- Craving for food when under pressure
- Frequent indigestion or heartburn
- Constipation or diarrhoea
- Insomnia
- Constant tiredness
- Tendency to sweat for no good reason
- Nervous twitches
- Nail biting
- Headaches
- Cramps and muscle spasms
- Nausea
- Breathlessness without exertion
- Fainting spells
- Frequent crying or desire to cry
- Impotency or frigidity
- Inability to sit still without fidgeting
- High blood pressure

Having one or more of the symptoms doesn't mean we are in dire and imminent peril. Other factors may be responsible, or the stress may be short term. However, inability to recognise a pattern of symptoms which are sustained over a longer period may mean we are failing in our duty to ourselves or to those significant others in our lives.

The cost of stress

Failing to do the right thing, and address workplace stress can result in a high cost to the individual and the business (Cooper and Dewe 2008). Aside from financial considerations, which we shall look at in a moment, there is the personal impact of unaddressed stress to consider. Here, there is no 'scale of suffering', where we can measure, in an objective sense, the damaging effects on the individual. However, where stress turns to anxiety or depression, it is self-evident that harm will come to the person involved and their immediate family and/or friends.

On this basis, managing stress must be on the agenda of any organisation that claims in its values, to be committed to corporate social responsibility and the wellbeing of their staff.

It is still the case where aggressive macho management cultures pay only lip service to such 'touchy-feely' principles, but if fair treatment of employees isn't high on the list of priorities, this should be overridden by the compelling business case, which outlines the financial cost of unaddressed stress.

The Confederation of British Industry has reported on the cost to industry of work-related stress for some years, stating sickness absence brought about by the affliction stood at half a million cases, the total cost of which amounted to £3.7 billion.

Estimates for the average length of time each stressed worker took off, stood at 29 days. The 'pattern' of these absences has not been tracked, but consider the effect it would have on the rest of the team if a co-worker was absent for a whole month. The prospect is no better if an absent/present/absent cycle pertains, where the stressed worker takes a few days off, feels better and returns, only to become stressed again. Estimates of total time lost in this way during 2004 stand at a massive 13 million working days.

And it gets worse. The serious long term repercussions of untreated stress can be life threatening, with 63,000 people in 2005 claiming work-related heart disease, exacerbated by chronic stress (Cooper et al 2009).

Absenteeism through stress is a factor which is much talked about, perhaps because it is tangible and can be measured. What is more insidious and tougher to track is presenteeism. Workers who display this trait are at work, despite not being fully fit, so they may be suffering the effects of stress, but continue to show up each day. This state of being in work, but not up to full capacity due to poor health, was named presenteeism by Hemp (2004), who went on to speculate the cost of this phenomenon could well be in excess of absenteeism.

It would be sensible to suggest that during the tough economic conditions we currently face, where many organisations are looking to lose people to reduce headcount and fixed cost, this issue will be worse than ever. No matter how philanthropic and compassionate the employer, we tend to think a 'survival of the fittest' rule pertains. So, as we have acknowledged already, an admission of not being able to cope may be seen as a sign of weakness and seal our fate. Furthermore, it is reasonable to believe under these circumstances, that the very fact of *having* to go to work, the place where our stress may be at it's height, would have the effect of causing even more stress.

Thus, it appears there are both 'push and pull' factors to suggest a change in the way staff are treated. A combination of positive action, in 'doing the right thing' is morally, and for many people individually, the 'best' course of action and the costs, financial and personal of not reducing 'unwell-being', are simply too high. Our advocacy of the right thing looks justifiable in this light.

Although we have examined some stress triggers, we have yet to analyse the issues a modern manager must cope with. In the next chapters, we look first at how the nature of work has evolved, before going on to consider some very real difficulties of managing today's workforce in a difficult and rapidly-changing commercial landscape.

Conclusions

The recognised constructs of stress can be influenced by individual managers

Stress is potentially damaging for us and the workers in our sphere of influence

There are a wide range of stress symptoms we can look out for

There is a moral case for stress reduction

Beyond simple good ethics, there is a financial case too – stress is costly

CHAPTER 4

The changing nature of the world of work

Wellbeing and happiness are desirable, but the workplace is a source of stress for many, robbing them of their opportunity to be as fulfilled as they might be. Has work always been this way, or has it's evolution over time made it a more stressful place? What are the big issues in work, and can we do anything about them?

We are constantly reminded that in work, change is constant, although this acceptance is from a modern school of thought. Some of the early theories of change management talked about it in terms of handling a single entity (i.e. moving from one fixed state to another). The truth is that the state we are moving *to* is constantly shifting, there is no 'fixed' element to it any more and even if we thought it so when the change started, by the time we get there, often the agenda will have moved on, rendering the 'fix' meaningless.

The Greek philosopher Heraclitus was an early exponent of the view that change is happening all the time. He stated, 'you can't stand in the same river twice'. So, as the waters of the workplace flow past (ever faster), if you step out of the stream, it will be different by the time you step back in, even if it's the same spot.

However, aside from clearly defined changes, like a departmental re-organisation, or an office move, which may still be seen as having a start and end point, the changes that occur are often imperceptible on a daily basis. It's a bit like watching your kids grow up. Day-to-day you see no change, but suddenly you'll catch yourself remembering something you used to do together, a visit to the park, a day on the beach and wonder where those times went. It's often hard even in retrospect to recall the 'moments in time' when things changed. When did you last tie their shoelaces for them, what was the last occasion when you pushed them on the swings?

In the workplace, the pace and dramatic nature of the changes that happen, strengthen the analogy still further. With child rearing, in the space of around 15 years, we go from providing all services, food, shelter, love, to becoming surplus to requirements (the usual parental jokes about being taxis and ATM's to their teenage progeny apply!).

The same dramatic alterations in the world of work occur in just as short a cycle, the imperatives that drive them are relentless and powerful, so what are the big things which are happening?

There are three distinct factors to consider here. Firstly, the changed nature of work due to globalisation; secondly, other significant and interrelated external factors which are part of operating in an inter-connected world, (see the forthcoming PEST analysis); and finally, the inexorable rise of media influence which has shrunk the planet.

Global business

The far-reaching effects of globalisation have never been more relevant than when applied to the workplace. Three major factors are at play; competition, time and culture. Let's take each one in order. The competitive nature of business on a world scale is not only important to large organisations. Labour costs, lower in poorer parts of the world, result in price reductions at the till, forcing domestic competition to cut margins. The retail picture is replicated across many sectors, and many organisations no longer feel they are on a level playing field.

Timescales too have reduced across the board, whether in the manufacturing process (bringing goods to market quicker), or in the development of new products (some electronic goods have only a 12 week product lifecycle, before a new model is launched). The nature of communication technology also means the world is 'always on'. There is never a point when one time zone or another is not working.

Finally, culture, particularly in terms of the strength of the work ethic, is affected. Pressure increases in those nations whose culture used to be more laconic (and therefore less stressed), to join the frantic high pressure world of their new competitors across on another continent.

The external and the uncontrollable

PEST (political, economic, sociological and technological) analysis is a commonly used tool for mapping external change forces and a useful way of summarising those influencers beyond our immediate control. It is also a dynamic form of analysis as the main headings it covers are ever changing in themselves.

The factors and their recent history are detailed below.

Political

The nature of this factor is that it is an overarching construct as long as we regard 'politics' as 'life'. What happens in the world on a daily basis, will have an impact on the political decisions of leaders and vice versa.

Staying in power is a key requirement of any regime, so moving with the flow and riding the punches is part of the agenda, whether that be in response to economic downturn or fighting terrorism. Stability is transient, especially when viewed across all the nations on earth. Unrest in the Middle East in 2011 spread quickly to many nations, and though the regime changes which were brought about, happened relatively swiftly, the further repercussions may play out over decades.

Economic

Managing the money within our own business is no longer enough. The financial state of our customers or suppliers is also of concern, if we are to be successful. Being part of a 'world economy' takes a lot of the control we may have once had, out of our hands. The sub prime mortgage collapse, which started in the U.S., soon began to have repercussions all around the world.

But as well as the downsides, there are also great opportunities too. Ebay, for example has given businesses a global platform to trade from, without measurably increasing costs. Expanding the potential customer base in this way has been the making of many online enterprises and entrepreneurs.

Sociological

National culture, information and choice are the three key elements that help to drive social attitudes, and the changes that rely on them. In the West, we have sought and continue to strive for greater equality in society, an eradication of unfairness and a longer term view of the world in relation to our impact on it's natural resources.

All of this comes at a price, either financial, or in terms of the effort we put in, so there is a continual balancing act of social changes against the resource needed to bring them about.

An example is ethical trading, which used to be thought of as something only indulged in by the well meaning green wellie brigade! It is now central to the mission of many organisations, and comes under the banner of corporate social responsibility (CSR).

Workplace demographics are changing too. There are two significant differences in the world of work today, compared to a generation ago. Firstly there are more women, and secondly, more older people.

The increase in the female working population is founded on a number of factors. Rising societal ambitions have meant lots of families aspire to a lifestyle, which a single income cannot fund. It is not just an increase in material wealth which people seek; often it is experiential in the form of more interesting family holiday destinations, or aspirational in other ways, say the funding of private education for the children of the family. In some cases, simply the rise in housing costs means both partners have to work in order to afford a roof over their heads.

The trend towards remaining single, and the increased incidence of divorce, has led to more women living alone, or at least without the support of a partner, necessitating a return to the workplace.

These social factors have increased the number of women in work, but a disparity still exists in the nature of the roles they take. Often the greater responsibility for child or elder care falls on the shoulders of women, meaning they have to balance work commitments with outside duties, resulting in them working part time, as a consequence they tend to be less well paid. The roles women take are influenced in part by these factors, and they tend towards public service roles, like administration, health and education as well as a significant proportion in hotels and catering. As future economic growth is dependent on the supply of highly skilled workers, and women are set to take the greater percentage of new roles created in the coming years, there is a need for organisations and individual managers to embrace policies which cater for their needs.

Over time, you can also expect as a manager to see an ageing population in the workplace. The 'secure' pension schemes of the past are just that, consigned to commercial history, and for many working people, staying on beyond 60 or 65 is no longer a matter of choice, but necessity.

The State has long campaigned for people to make more of their own provision and, as a consequence, pensions have fallen in real terms, forcing many to remain in the workplace in order to get by.

The trend towards an older workforce is set to continue, according to Dixon (2003), 'older workers will, in time, constitute a larger share of the labour force than in recent history'. This too will mean new challenges in constructing work which is meaningful for older workers, preserving their knowledge in the organisation and implementing policies which may allow for more flexible hours.

Technological

The far reaching effects of changes in technology affect every aspect of business and society. Three major areas of development are speed, availability and communication.

Virtually everything we now do, we do faster, old rules about the availability of goods, services and people have been trashed as we have become a 24/7 world. All this is enabled by a proliferation of new communication channels that allow data, in a multitude of formats, to be squirted around the globe at the speed of light.

The influence of the media

We have reserved a special place for 'media' in our analysis of the factors that influence change in the workplace. The reason for this is the media's ability to report and comment on *all* the other factors; it is woven like a thread throughout them. The significance of the way we are now communicated to, (or at) has a life all of its' own.

Let us examine some of the effects of this interlacing of media influence within the major external factors to change.

Politics and media are tied closer together than ever, as individual careers and even the reputations of whole governments, can be irreparably damaged overnight. From the sex scandal surrounding a Senator or Member of Parliament, through to a failure to deal with a fiscal or defence issue, the repercussions can be magnified by a baying media to deafening proportions, sometimes resulting in, or at the very least, contributing to downfall.

We might be drawn towards the belief that this is a good thing, as investigative journalists seek to uncover wrongdoing at an individual or institutional level, and the history of the profession has shown us many fine examples of brave reporting in the face of tremendous pressure to stay silent.

Indeed, this argument about 'in the public interest' is the catchall used by editors across the piece from newspapers through the spectrum of broadcast media, to justify both the methods employed and the causes that are championed.

A more cynical viewpoint suggests this role as 'guardian of public good and morality' is used as a smokescreen to cloak the fact that some stories are pursued purely for salacious reasons, and that their content, which appeals to the base voyeurism in all of us, sells papers, or boosts audience.

If we have a personal point of view on where the line in the sand is drawn, this is much less relevant than recognising the power at play. Going back to the politicians, they know a story can make or break them. If they can exercise influence over the media in a proactive way, it's less likely they'll be caught out over a negative story, so this is one of the areas they put their greatest efforts.

Even relatively minor indiscretions or slips of the tongue can fuel a story which will run for days, usually attracting the suffix of 'gate', after the famous Watergate scandal. Political figures remain tight-lipped over their personal preferences (do they smoke, or drink?), their beliefs (religious or atheist?) and their past (did they take drugs at university?), but this is exactly the kind of information some journalists like to pursue.

Sometimes, defence is the best form of attack, so it's often the case that one political party will spend their resources in finding ammunition to use against its' opponents, 'spin doctoring' their side of the story to the media. When this behaviour escalates the result has been dubbed 'Punch and Judy' politics, a kind of tit-for-tat knockabout, where there is rarely a clear winner.

One potentially damaging aspect of the media in politics is the speed of change, which can render a story 'worthless' in a matter of minutes, following a sustained period where it was front page news. If there is nothing to fuel the flames of a scandal, no new information, then a new 'scoop' will take its place. This is sometimes referred to as 'Drop the Dead Donkey', a reference to putting an end to one story, to concentrate on the next.

How politics impacts on our world of work

So how does all this sensitivity to the media agenda on the part of politicians affect the workplace? Here are a few examples that might help illustrate the bigger picture.

During times of harsh economic conditions, governments will need to cut expenditure and this is bound to impact on public services. However, where the cuts fall and who has to bear the brunt of the harshest ones, is likely to be influenced by the potential damaging stories that could follow.

This has meant in the U.K. that the National Health Service was initially ring-fenced; people dying as a direct result of not getting the care they needed because funds were not available, makes for grim reading, especially for the politicians. The reality is that life and death decisions are made on a daily basis, sometimes in a tacit, rather than deliberate way, simply because there is not enough resource to provide everyone with every medical intervention, but any newspaper trying to sell a story to us is unlikely to point that out.

How a government divides a dwindling pot of money has a massive effect on many thousands of public sector workers. It potentially damages their 'benefits' and adds insecurity to their futures. There is a knock-on effect too for private sector organisations, many of which rely on government-funded bodies as a significant part of their customer base.

Politics and economics can be seen to be closely linked in this way and it would be naive to think this picture is not influenced (and sometimes manipulated), by media reporting.

The wider sociological agenda can be at the beck and call of a bad news story too. The so called 'legal high' mephedrone was banned in 2010 in the U.K., as a result of a news story which suggested that two teenage boys had died after taking the drug. In the lead up to a General Election, the government of the day could not be seen to be soft on drugs, although it was later shown that the boys had taken a cocktail of alcohol and other drugs, making it impossible to say that the mephedrone had been solely responsible for their deaths. Whether the drug would have been banned had the media not pursued the story is questionable and this is another example of the power they wield.

It is not unusual for the media to extrapolate a single case (of anything), and lead an uninformed public into believing that a situation is worse than it may really be. Pandemic scares, binge drinking and violent crime are all fodder for this kind of treatment, leaving us unsure of whether things really are getting worse or not.

These two examples illustrate the power of the media in political, economic and sociological spheres, even the financial confidence of a nation can be affected by negative reports on high street spending, sending the spiral ever downwards.

Finally, the media can probably be said to have less effect on technology than the impact technology has on it.

Social networking, video phones and twitter have all contributed to 'news by the people' with breaking stories often being supplemented by amateur footage or debates being influenced and shaped by viewer opinion, captured in real time.

We can conclude that a wide range of factors from global markets, through external influences to media input have altered the landscape of work immeasurably and irreversibly. Just to survive, we have often been tempted to do the *wrong* thing. Before we examine how to start the process of redressing the balance, let us consider in the next chapter what workplace behaviours now look like.

Conclusions

Change is happening all the while, often incrementally and imperceptibly

It's not just international businesses which are affected by globalisation

The factors outside our control are dynamic and ever changing

Media influence runs like a thread through many change drivers

CHAPTER 5

Three management issues

Coping with change is one thing, but the task of management is made even more complicated by some of the ongoing issues which have become embedded in many workplaces. The degree to which your organisation suffers from these will be down to many factors, including its size, type and culture. This final element governs a host of behaviours in the workplace, and we will return to it for further analysis and discussion later.

Issue 1   Workplace rules devised for 'exceptions'

The problem with many workplaces is that they are over burdened by rules. Some important aspects of what we do need to be defined, for the benefit of both parties to the contract, so it's to be expected that the parameters of the working day are laid out, as well as the broad outline of expectation with regard to job function. The difficulty seems to be that we don't know where to stop.

Of course, the growing body of legislation covering workplace activities hasn't helped in this regard, and though it's important to take account of health and safety or diversity, it is not so much the ethos of the law which makes life difficult, but the weighty, time consuming, bureaucratic execution which gives it such a bad name.

This shift seems to have brought with it a 'life by the rulebook' attitude to many businesses, so in order to avoid any potentially 'bad' situation companies put in place a rule. Often though, this is for the exceptional circumstance, to cover every eventuality rather than the norm, leaving managers burdened by bureaucracy.

Lynn – HR Manager

'It's an attractive company Nokia, a real success story, so we got used to people from other industries getting in touch and asking for the "royal tour", it was something we were happy to do.

On one occasion I was showing a senior executive from another company around and we stopped for a cup of coffee in the staff restaurant. There was the normal collection of regular staff and "creatives" in there, the latter dressed in their usual outlandish way. The visitor leant over and asked me in a conspiratorial whisper 'what's the dress code here at Nokia?'

I just laughed and told him, we don't have a dress code. We think people are sensible enough to know what to wear. If it's a formal business meeting they dress smartly, otherwise it's up to them. He looked horrified. It's laughable though, organisations make rules "just in case" to cover exceptions. By the nature of that, it doesn't apply to most people, most of the time, so why do it?'

Consider your own business, and think about where it stands on rule making, are there proscriptive practices laid down to cover every eventuality, or is there an expectation staff will behave in a responsible way for most of the time?

Some managers operate on the basis that 'if you give them an inch, they'll take a mile' so zero tolerance becomes the order of the day and to administer this, a supporting rule book evolves. How then do we win over those whose belief is based on 'prevention'? It seems from the Nokia example the dress code issue is cultural, people know what is acceptable and what is not, so perhaps this is the starting point for breaking down rule-based dictatorships, the culture needs to shift.

The history of business has its part to play here too. A couple of generations ago the order of the day was a strict hierarchy, and a set of management behaviours to support it. Workers were treated in a 'lowest common denominator' fashion, given little flexibility and expected to do things by the book. All well and good when you need clarity, but more persuasive and coercive behaviours have crept into modern management, where workers are kept 'on side' by being inclusive, rather than directive. Nokia is a relatively young company, which may explain it's enlightened attitude in this regard. We would probably all benefit from taking a leaf out of their book.

Issue 2 Emotional territorialism

In some sense, nearly all disputes are over territory. Nations fight each other over where a boundary is drawn, neighbours fall out over trees planted on *their* side of the line, but territory isn't always physical. Sometimes territory can be emotional too, like in the example of the firstborn, seeking to regain ground after a sibling arrives, or the friendships of teenage girls who drift in and out of liaisons daily.

In work environments too, people fall out over what they perceive is a lack of parity. One worker seems to get treated better by the boss because their emotional capital is higher (a bit like being teacher's pet at school). The complexities that surround this situation are immense. Side with the 'pet' in an attempt to be in with the in-crowd, be part of the rebellious alliance (your complaining co-workers), or sit on the fence hoping to be able to make a decision on which way to jump as you witness the unfolding situation?

The concept of 'competition' can be a force for good in the workplace, often we have no choice but to compete with other suppliers in the market place. At best a healthy quest for self-improvement prevails. However, when this strategy fails, some feel the only way to gain competitive advantage is to diminish the offer your adversary is making. The resultant negativity can be damaging to both parties.

With one-to-one relationships the same rule applies. If we are head-to-head with a colleague to hit a target or achieve promotion, there is a positive motivational force behind both of us. But if we begin to lose ground, see our territory being eaten away, we might resort to negative tactics to bring them down, effectively give them a metaphorical dig in the ribs when no one is looking.

This situation is much exacerbated by the tacit approval of an organisation, which rewards 'winners' and ignores the rest. The behaviour is more or less prevalent according to where you are working, both by industry type and geographically; contrast, for example, the level of competition felt between colleagues on a village farm collective or the investment banking arm of a City institution.

We need to be careful not to judge competition as a 'bad' thing. But to ignore it's potential for destruction of relationships, of trust and ultimately perhaps even of people, is a risky strategy indeed.

As a manager we need to stay attuned to the competition within our teams, let it thrive when positive outcomes occur, but be prepared to intervene if things turn nasty.

Issue 3   Motivation and the drive for high performance

The individual friction between our own work relationships can sometimes be the result of our bosses pitting us against one another.

And part of the reason for doing this stems from our third workplace issue, the drive for high performance.

So endemic is this, in many organisations, managers have ceased to question its long term benefits or validity. It is the kind of 'now' culture, which if persisted with day after day can lead to harmful stress. The drive is no longer just for greater productivity; it's also for this slightly more intangible 'high performance', a kind of holy grail for managers, seeking to squeeze the last ounce of 'can do' attitude from their staff.

The great advantage of 'people' is that though we class them in the workplace as an amorphous mass, 'we value our people', 'people are our greatest asset', they are in truth all individuals and as such, feel, think and behave slightly differently from each other. The brain scientist Professor Susan Greenfield enthusiastically espouses the uniqueness of each of us (CIPD annual conference, 2003). If we stop to consider this for a moment, it is truly amazing that no one else on the planet can ever think the thoughts or feel the experiences we do. Every action we take, every experience we have or sensation we feel, we process in a different way to others.

Is this always an advantage though? What looks like a real bonus on the one hand, can also have an opposite and counter balancing effect on the other. Because each member of the team is 'different', any action, decision or directive we introduce as a manager, will have a slightly altered impact on every individual, making achievement of high performance difficult. By logical extension, any motivational theory or application can only at best be considered a 'shotgun' rather than a 'rifle', unless that is, the translation and communication of the 'motivator' (more flexible working, greater responsibility, hard cash), is handled by a manager and *translated* for staff on an individual basis.

If we go for an obvious motivator like money, we can easily understand that each member of the team might perceive it differently. For one, it may mean paying off a credit card, reducing some of the stress associated with debt, for another it could be the opportunity to fund an indulgence, like flying lessons. Yet another might see it as a way of giving their children a more memorable Christmas, so the 'shotgun' has a positive effect on all three, but in very different ways.

The reality of what happens in many organisations is 'high performance' comes and goes. To begin with, it's not something that can happen in isolation from the outside world. In retail, for example, a sharp downturn in sales can act as a catalyst to an un-virtuous circle, with managers becoming demoralised, putting more pressure on staff, who in turn become 'depressed' by the situation, risking a change in attitude towards customers.

No longer the cheery greeting upon entering the store; the usual smiling faces at the checkout have been replaced by an altogether more sombre look, and it's just not as nice a place to shop any more, so the circle is complete and performance in both individual and organisational terms continues in it's downward spiral.

In all of this example, we haven't considered how staff and managers were performing right at the start, as sales fell. They may have been working as hard as ever, but factors outside their control meant earlier success couldn't be sustained.

If external influencers, like an economic downturn can affect the business, so too can some of the internal decisions that are taken in response to this. A change in senior management, followed by a move away from core business as the organisation attempts to diversify, exacerbated by poor buying decisions, resulting in goods in store which consumers reject, can all have a major impact on the success of the enterprise. There is nothing those at operational level can do about it, at least not on a day-to-day basis.

People who are at the customer interface don't necessarily change in character, but their individual and collective mood can be swayed by either good or bad news, exactly the same as in our private lives. When this happens and 'high performance' turns to 'average performance', either the organisation has to batten down the hatches and wait for the storm, economic or otherwise, to blow over, or it has to be brave and attempt to inject some impetus to swing the mood back the other way.

But we're in danger here of falling into our own trap and treating the workforce as the 'amorphous mass' referred to earlier. Surely as individuals, people can express themselves without reference to the herd? For many this proves impossible, so instead of swimming against the tide of opinion, they get sucked into the maelstrom of negativity.

It is here that great leaders begin to emerge. These people may not be solely confined to the top management tiers of the organisation. 'Mood leaders' can be at any level, the cheery, indefatigable hotel concierge, the chipper sales assistant, the whistling warehouseman. These are the people who can make a huge difference to the morale of the workforce as a whole.

As Mark Twain wrote, 'keep away from people who try to belittle your ambitions, small people always do that, but the really great make you feel that you, too, can somehow become great'.

Companies lucky enough to have an abundance of this type are less likely to suffer in poor market conditions, because the personal resilience of a rump of their staff comes to represent the corporate resilience of the organisation as a whole.

These 'keep calm and carry on' types are the stuff of great companies.

Conclusions

Today's managers face a legacy of work-based problems which are ingrained

A rulebook can be good or evil, according to who is writing it

Relationships and personalities make up much of a manager's working day

In spite of these difficulties, we seem to be expected to deliver more for less

De-motivators are often outside our control, but we have to deal with the fallout

CHAPTER 6

Three sources of toxicity

A blank sheet of paper, that's what we would all like when we start a new management role, but life is never that simple. Instead we parachute into an established organisation, and do our best to deal with the baggage it is dragging along.

We conclude our look at the difficulties managers face by examining a further three elements of many modern workplaces.

1. Mediocrity – why organisations tolerate it

If we think of business as a battle, then our foot soldiers are fighting the good fight on a daily basis across a number of fronts. These might included economic conditions on a local, national or global scale, competition, societal change, customer preference, rising service expectations, all of which are legitimate and long running themes. The route to success is to attempt to overcome these pitfalls, better, faster, often cheaper than anyone else.

If all of this weren't enough to cope with, our steadfast troops have also to contend with an enemy within. A collection of 'toxic individuals', sometimes known as 'the well poisoners', whose behaviour ranges from the apathetic, through the obstructive, all the way to the saboteur in extreme cases. Why then aren't these traitors rooted out and forced to leave, so that the rest of the workforce can concentrate on winning the battles that matter?

Is it that they're hard to spot? Do they go underground and disguise themselves as 'good' soldiers? Hardly, in fact in any team that contains such a destructive force, everyone else is able to point them out and cite the reasons why they are so bad for morale. It's important we acknowledge we aren't talking about poor performance which may be allied to a lack of skill or experience, after all both these things can be redressed with effort and investment over time. Instead, we're referring to the kind of negative attitude which results in a complete withdrawal of good will, a determination to only do the minimum, a lack of engagement with the aims and objectives of the company.

Curiously, these workers often feel part of a team, but usually fail to see that they are any different from their peers. If their 'toxicity' were limited to just their own job role, they would be slightly more tolerable, but usually they aren't content with this and feel the need to spread their message of doom to anyone who will listen. They are the 'this bloody company' merchants, the 'what do you expect from management like ours' types, we've all met them.

An added difficulty of carrying people is when the going gets tough, they are even more of a problem. In good times, when their presence can be afforded but ignored, those around them tend to plough on regardless. However, when facing cut-backs and redundancies their colleagues are often up in arms. If the dead wood were cut from the organisation, the remaining hard workers would be more secure.

So why do organisations continue to tolerate these people?

Here are some reasons:

Led by example – the uncomfortable truth for many senior managers or Board Directors is their peers might not all be pulling their weight. If this is the case and poor performance at the top level is not addressed, it sends a signal to all those below in the organisation which says, 'it's okay to ignore this'. A Finance Director who gets the numbers wrong or a Head of Marketing who second guesses a product or service badly, need to be seen to have some sanction imposed upon them. After all, these are the people charged with providing the strategic direction of the organisation, so if they can't get it right, what hope is there for the rest of us?

Employment law – legislation aimed at protecting the rights of the individual against the might of the corporation are generally seen to be a good thing. No one should suffer corporate bullying, having conditions of service changed on a whim, or their services disposed of in an equally light fashion. However the protection afforded to the genuine hard worker also shields the 'disengaged'. In many organisations today, managers will privately tell you it's impossible to get rid of anyone. Often, the 'toxic' workers we're talking about here have amassed an encyclopaedic knowledge of the relevant parts of employment law in order to keep themselves protected.

They'll know how many 'sick' days they can take before their case gets looked at closely, their understanding of grievance procedure would put a barrister to shame. If they put the same amount of effort into working as they do to finding ways of avoiding it, they would surely have a meteoric rise through the ranks of the company.

Effort and stress – The weight of protection afforded to individuals, often supported and backed by a trade union, leads many managers to back away from the problem of poor performance. Doing the right thing means taking the issue on, but with it comes a lot of procedural effort associated with the organisation's disciplinary format (verbal warning, written warning, setting and monitoring of performance standards, etc.). Alongside this, the manager has to be able to 'prove' parity, i.e. the individual has not been singled out for this kind of attention and their performance really is being judged on the same criteria as their peers.

This sounds time consuming, and it is. But that's not even the half of it, because in almost all circumstances, the negative associations behind this kind of management, allied to the often difficult face-to-face meetings with the individual in question, often result in very high levels of personal stress for the manager. We have heard cases of managers not sleeping for several nights before such a meeting, or finding themselves angry and irritable, both with their other members of staff and in the domestic environment. It's maybe not surprising that so few seem to be prepared to take these situations on.

Self interest – 'outsider syndrome' is that feeling we all get from time to time which says we're just 'getting away with this'. A sense that any day now, someone is going to tap us on the shoulder and say, 'okay, your time's up, we've got your number'. There's nothing wrong with having a little insecurity in work, it keeps us sharp and prevents the kind of arrogance that can lead to poor decision making. However, it also makes us unwilling to unbalance the status quo. Whatever happens, we don't want anyone rocking the boat.

In the same way that turkeys might avoid voting for Christmas, so too do workers fight shy of having a forensic examination of their operational efficiency. Who then would advocate that the 'inspectors' should be invited to come crawling all over the organisation? And these can come in many forms, auditors, consultants, government appointed bodies, maybe even a head office team coming to visit our regional outpost.

So, our natural self-protection leads us towards a position where we don't like too many questions to be asked, which provides yet another hiding place. It's a further barrier to outsiders, which helps to protect those who are letting the side down.

It is often convenient to sweep mediocrity under the carpet, but the plain truth is the loss of effort from those not pulling their weight is just the tip of the iceberg. Below the waterline a toxicity spreads throughout the remainder of the workforce, whose resentment and dissatisfaction over 'a problem ignored' fights at direct odds with any motivational strategies you seek to pursue.

If we're not careful, mediocrity will be here to stay, unless some of us are brave enough to stand up for the right thing. Not all poor performers are irredeemable though and we have to carefully sort the lost causes from the simply de-motivated.

The next section looks at how some people became so disengaged in the first instance.

2. The un-work ethic

Prejudice, bias, core beliefs and life experience often coalesce to form our view of the world and never more so than in the workplace. Douglas McGregor (1960), took an interesting polarised view of management when outlining his Theory X and Theory Y of motivation.

Provide the workforce with the right environment to do their best work, encourage and empower them, and you can leave them to get on with it, according to Theory Y managers that is. On the contrary, their opposite numbers at the Theory X end of the scale, harbour the belief that workers are feckless wasters who need to be directed, yelled at and threatened in order to get them to do anything meaningful.

Where does the truth lie?

Most modern managers get the whole 'emotional intelligence' thing, they understand in order to keep your troops onside, you need to apply a little empathy, show you care about them as people and engage them in decision-making. But are they applying a technique, while secretly harbouring a Theory X belief system? And if this is the case, where does it come from?

In praise of laziness

Hard pressed managers, stressed by the burden put upon them by their employers, will find it frankly offensive if we suggest that 'laziness' is inherent in humans and endemic in the work-place, so some explanation of the term is needed.

What we're talking about in this context is a 'natural reserve, a holding back of some energy and effort, a not-giving-your-all, the evidence for which is all around us. Resistance to 'time and motion' studies in the workplace was a direct result of people not wanting their 'potential for efficiency' measured. Much better it remained uncharted, a personal secret for us (the work-force) to know, and you (the management) to guess.

A lovely comedic example of this 'holding back' is played out in an early Tom Hanks movie, 'Big', where Hanks, as the central character goes from 12 year old boy to fully grown man overnight (via a fairground 'grant-your-wish' machine). Soon he finds himself in the workplace, and is berated by a colleague for working too fast. In his still childlike mind, he figures the best way to get through the day is to do the work as quickly as possible, his colleagues had 'learned' otherwise.

As with so much of our behaviour in a work context, this is very much fuelled by organisational culture. If you've been employed by a variety of companies, you will be able to draw your own comparisons over how hard people worked in each, in relative terms.

Here are some reasons why it happens:

Control

Even when we accept hierarchy as a part of working life, we still like to be in a position of exercising some control over what we do, rather than have every single action dictated to us by our immediate superior. Mundane jobs still usually have a degree of choice in them, maybe over the order in which things are done, the method employed, or perhaps the thoroughness or speed required.

It matters to our wellbeing to be able to do this, as we discussed earlier when looking at stress.

Pace yourself

Remember when you were a child and took to the sports field? At first we simply can't resist the temptation to run around like mad things, chasing the ball all over the pitch, but soon we come to realise that it's a long game, and we need to conserve some energy for later. A similar thing happens at work, where we anticipate future busy periods, and save a little of our energy for when they occur.

One difficulty in the modern workplace is that we rarely get to set the pace any more. The agenda is much more likely to be driven by those above us. Soon, the exceptional performance we put in under pressure (like that burst of energy when you sprinted full pelt down the wing), becomes the expected norm.

The 'more' factor

Whatever you do, they'll ask you for 'more'. Imagine you're a manager who was once just one of the team. In the old days, you didn't shirk, but what you did fit into what was generally regarded as a normal working pattern, defined by those around you. Now you've been promoted, you know that the capacity of those in your charge is greater than they are currently putting in. Although you're not able to calibrate this accurately, if you keep asking for more, you'll eventually find out where the limit of their capacity and ability is.

Tipping the balance

We view our contracts of employment, both written and implicit, as a charter for how much work is expected from us, and the level of remuneration that attracts. Many things go to govern this 'norm', not least the historical origins of the role, but also today, more than ever, market forces.

Many people have called into question, particularly in recent recessionary times, how one person can be paid an hourly rate as a banker, which equates to the *weekly* wage of another. How can one person's value be so much more? Sports stars too have come under the spotlight, while the rest of society is burdened by austerity measures, an elite few are earning a fortune.

So, 'fairness' is relative, but we are likely to benchmark ourselves against similar roles in associated industries. Having made this comparison, none of us wants to be taken for a fool. If we work too hard, we'll simply be giving more than our employer bargained for.

3. Managing through austerity

Although we've already mentioned the difficult economic climate, it is worth examining in a little more detail what managing in austerity means for managers.

Whatever workplace issues we might face, there is no getting away from the blight on our efforts brought about by harsh economic conditions. When managers have to do their jobs with less resource, life gets harder for everyone. If we assume the workload doesn't diminish, it may be that reducing the headcount saves money, but the work is re-distributed among the survivors of the redundancy sweep.

This is only part of the impact on the greater workforce. Many organisations are bringing in pay freezes for two or three years. The most obvious effect of this is that in real terms, staff are facing a pay cut, as the worth of their salaries is eroded by inflation.

In many organisations there is a deeper psychological impact of the pay freeze. In the past workers who got scant feedback from their managers had one piece of good news coming their way each year, a pay increase. In some instances, this would be the only indication that they were on the map, doing a good job and deserving of recognition.

Now, our already time starved managers have little to give away, making them more reluctant than ever to offer feedback, and as a consequence, the opportunity for recognition is dwindling alongside the self-worth of the workforce.

Add to this the longer term worries brought about by austerity measures, and the picture is indeed bleak. We spend much of our working lives with an eye to retirement. None of us wants a pauper's grave, but with cut backs resulting in changes to pension schemes, it seems our worries might not just be confined to today, but to the far future as well.

Conclusions

Poor performance affects everyone, and is getting harder to manage

The law protects disengaged workers, but they're usually quite adept too

What some see as laziness is often self-protection

Austerity ratchets up the pressure on managers, everything is more difficult

CHAPTER 7

An appearance of greener grass

We have looked at a number of common issues in the workplace, but the emphasis on them can differ according to whether they are applied in the public or private sector. So, we propose to compare and contrast how opposing organisational cultures attract different kinds of people to work within them, and to consider the differing stressors which might apply in each category.

Although it's impossible to typify all organisations in a few paragraphs, there are some major differences between the public and private sector which have a bearing on how they do their 'business', and the effect that this might have on the wellbeing of their people.

There is often envy between the two categories, each one thinking the other has it easier. So is the grass really greener on the other side, or is it the proverbial 'trick of the light'?

Public service

The type of people who are drawn to the public sector can often be recognised by looking at the values, functions and the operations of such organisations. What we often find is a spread of different types of individuals, who share a common vision, not only of how their employer operates, but how the world at large functions.

Often these are people for who work acts as a vocational calling. Their value and belief system has at its core a sense of social justice, a desire to make the world a better, fairer, safer place for all members of society, irrespective of background. An admin assistant at your local council office may not spring to mind, but how about a prison chaplain, a nurse or a social worker? There is a general belief that people in this kind of role have a relationship with their employer which goes beyond a straight swap of effort in exchange for remuneration.

The psychological contract between employer and employee tends to have greater depth in the public sector, as staff are more wedded to the ideals of the organisation. In the private sector, loyalty still exists, but the underpinning ethos of the company tends to owe more to market forces than philanthropy, which means a very different 'contract' pertains.

One major area of difference between the sectors is in the 'disengaged' population they carry with them. These are people who for a host of reasons have become de-motivated, turn up only for the money and do the least they can get away with (see Chapter 6).

Generally speaking the public sector holds a more benevolent attitude to its staff. On the up side, this means more effort is put into parity of treatment, compassionate policies and empathy with the needs of the individual.

The corresponding downside is this can lead mediocre performers to simply 'hang on in there'. Anecdotally, public sector managers complain vociferously about such staff, and it seems they have a greater number of them to deal with. In our discussions with managers in both sectors, we noticed the same issues cropping up again and again. Here are some difficulties public sector managers have to cope with.

Bad management

Because there is often the aforementioned vocational calling with public sector roles, the people who work there are often hyper-critical of internal policy which is at odds with the worthy aims of the organisation. The health sector is a prime example, where front line staff view 'middle managers' as a waste of time and money, contributing nothing to patient care, but costing the organisation dearly.

A deeper investigation would most likely prove waste or mismanagement has always been a part of life in such an organisation, and the addition of new managers with a more commercial outlook was originally designed to fix this problem. It then becomes difficult to judge when this has gone too far, and 'over management' begins to take place.

Politics

When it comes to political influence, successive governments seem unsure about how much power to devolve to a local level, and this often results in one re-organisation after another, de-stabilising systems and processes while increasing the stress upon people who have to learn new ways of working. For example, you will hear people complaining about a new I.T. system, saying that the previous one was 'perfectly good...why did it have to change?' Memories are short though, and if you could spool back to the time when the old system was in place, there were probably just as many complaints about it.

Poor performance

As such a large employer, it is clear through the law of averages the public sector will be 'carrying' a percentage of under-performers, which we discussed earlier. Part of the difficulty for these organisations is their policies, inherent sense of fairness and the kind of compassionate caring people they tend to attract, all act as significant barriers to dealing with the issue.

How do you deal with an employee who is depressed or has an alcohol problem? Put performance measures in place and effectively manage them out of the organisation, or turn a blind eye and hope it will resolve itself over time? Of course, underperformance is a broader issue than this, but nonetheless the point is valid.

Private sector

If the private sector has been the sole area of your working life, you may be unaware that many of your public sector counterparts view you with a mixture of envy and puzzlement! The general feeling is that private companies are more aggressive in the pursuit of their ends. As we have identified, profit is often at the heart of this, and a necessary part of most privately owned organisations. During tough economic times, this is all about survival.

This tends to mean the room for 'dead wood' is considerably less Every employee not pulling their weight is a burden on the bottom line, and it is profit which sustains survival.

Because this equation is plain and simple for all to see, it results in employees feeling indignation, injustice and frustration over the poor performance of colleagues. The imperative for managers to take action, not only to address the issue, but to save face, is usually strong enough to ensure that something is done.

Other important themes emerged when we spoke to private sector managers and these are summarised below.

Blame

Far too few companies really live their values. Often what is espoused as organisational ethos turn out to be nothing more than aspiration. As well as 'blame', 'risk' is another area where management say one thing but react differently when things go wrong.

Generally speaking, the workforce likes to know where it stands. Even if this is sometimes unpalatable, it is better than living in a confused state where rules are constantly changing. Organisations that give clear, consistent messages tend to be better managed, and there is less stress.

Targets

Productivity and efficiency are at the heart of a profitable business, so it is sometimes inevitable that leaders ask for more, often with less resource. Many organisations are fitter and leaner for this, but there is a finite limit to do more with less and some industries have a reputation for 'burning people out'. The rewards they offer are high, but few can last the pace in the longer term.

If you know this at the start then the bargain is a fair one, but often people sign up not understanding just how much sustained pressure they are going to face. The personal consequences can be devastating.

Technology

In the 70s, when mobile phones were new, they were seen as a status symbol. Now most of us have rumbled the fact that when we're given a Blackberry to 'enable' us, it means we can always be contacted, 24-7!

Individual managers carry a weight of responsibility here, because their behaviour can set the tone for the team, but it's not unknown, not even rare for workers to be sent email in the early hours of the morning. Even if we're in bed and don't reply, we probably stress about it as soon as we wake and see 'message waiting'.

Contrasting stressors of each sector

This analysis is broad brush, but designed to show the different potential sources of stress according to sector. The reason for this is to gain an understanding of what might need 'fixing' in each case, if we are aiming to change behaviours and 'do the right thing'.

The qualitative evidence we have gathered suggests some main themes which lead to stress, although there is strong empirical evidence as well (Lundberg and Cooper 2010).

There are pros and cons to wherever we work, but it is probably fair to say the stresses are equal; they simply come from different sources.

'Show me the money'

People are often prepared to put up with a degree of stress, it they believe the rewards they receive compensate for it. When it comes to remuneration, the widely held view is the private sector is better paid, but overall, the financial rewards even out in the long term, as public sector pension schemes have traditionally been better.

We would contend that financial comparisons are not nearly this simple. As workers in each sector are asked to do such different jobs, in environments so dissimilar, a true comparison is virtually impossible. If we accept too that there is a trade off in our chosen job role, it is even harder to compare one organisation or sector with another. How do we put a monetary value on things like security of tenure, organisational integrity, parity and fairness?

Wherever we choose to work, it is usually a reflection not just of our skill set and experience, but also our personality. However, when it comes to stress, whether you have opted for pubic or private sector there is no longer anywhere to hide!

Conclusions

There is often a vocational element to public sector work

Pressure in the private sector is most likely to come from the profit ethic

Job security used to be greater in public organisations, recession may have changed this

Irrespective of their aims, organisations can cause their staff to be stressed in pursuit of them

CHAPTER 8

Enough about them – what about you?

We have seen, through an examination of some of the common problems in business how difficult the life of a manager can be, but at the same time, how it can be highly rewarding when we get it right. Before we look at some strategies that can be employed, it is essential to understand the person who will be implementing them. It is important to reflect on who 'you' are as a manager, and what makes 'you' work the way you do. In doing this, let us first consider the impact you, as a manager can have on your staff, both good and bad.

We might readily speculate that bad management has a negative effect on the mental wellbeing of our staff, it's common sense. Although scientific studies have already validated what we may have thought, it is the *extent* to which employees are affected which is really surprising (Rayner et al 2002).

Poor management has been shown to lead to a variety of negative consequences across a spectrum, from helplessness (Ashforth 1994), through stress (Richman et al 1992), eventually to anxiety and depression.

Sustained over time, these management behaviours can lead to negative wellbeing effects beyond the boundaries of the workplace (Tepper 2000), so life satisfaction is reduced and work-family conflict increases.

But what many may regard as 'low level abuse' is seen to have significant impact on the recipients of the bad management practice; examples include 'not giving credit where due', 'being rude' or 'making negative comments about an employee to others'. Perhaps for some, this kind of 'abuse' may have typified their school days, and they believed they'd left it behind when they entered the world of work. Maybe the reality is we are not very good at dealing with criticism, but whatever the outcome, the catalyst is often a poor manager.

On the contrary, the positive effect we can have is heartening. Bass (1997), talked of transformational leadership and cited 4 contributing behaviours, namely 'idealised influence', (meaning good moral and ethical conduct), 'inspirational motivation', 'intellectual stimulation' and 'individual consideration'. When employees are treated in this way, lower levels of anxiety were found. Interestingly this 'good wellbeing' had a knock on effect in encouraging more of the positive management behaviour, so a virtuous circle is created (Van Dierendonck et al 2004).

Many things drive our success as managers, so let us consider two aspects, rational behaviour and risk behaviour.

Rational behaviour

How do organisations grow and prosper, what is it within your job role that contributes to the success of your enterprise? These are the kind of questions which analysts, accountants, marketers and consultants have sought the answer to since business management became a conscious process and professional discipline.

The history of commerce is littered with success stories from engineering to I.T., from retail to manufacturing. Great people have had the foresight, the determination and the will to bring about change, gain competitive advantage or engineer societal improvement on the basis of their visionary policy. As Albert Einstein once remarked, 'imagination is more important than knowledge'.

That's the positive inspirational bit which we all seek to engage with, but it is also a rarity. The reality of working life is that for most of us, for most of the time, success is a much vaguer, more tenuous concept. It is made all the more ethereal by the fact there is no finite end point. Leading organisations don't suddenly arrive at 'success junction'; and think 'the job is done'.

Business and life are much more dynamic, so success is harder to judge, we sort of know what it's based on, but there is no silver bullet. In the main, there is no charismatic, visionary madman leading the charge into a bright new future. Instead, there are some clever, well meaning and often 'safe' managers, doing what's been done before and occasionally trying something different. But only a little bit different.

This is not intended as a criticism of the way managers operate. In fact it is this very process of 'farming', keeping the thing ticking along, which has ensured security, steady growth and alignment with core values for many organisations. Solidity isn't about changing course every five minutes.

Leading brands provide us with a good example. If we chart the change in their relative market strength over time, we find that dominant products from decades ago, are often still in the same position of strength today. Over a 50 year period the 'presentation' of these products will have changed, packaging design will have evolved in line with other trends, maybe even the formulation of some lines will have altered, but in a modern supermarket, we are most likely buying some 'standard' products that our mothers, even grandmothers bought before us.

Organisations need 'farmers'. People who will maintain the status quo, with a safe pair of hands and the intelligence to observe what's happening in the market combined with the energy to see the slow but constant evolution of their core purpose. All of this, needs to be combined with a healthy slice of luck and an enduring resilience.

The public sector is no different. If anything it is even safer and slower in its incremental changes. The role public servants perform is often more complex in terms of 'reading the runes', as it's not just the measure of market share that they must take account of. Their key indicators are often more tenuous, in the form of public opinion, societal and demographic change and response to economic conditions on a local to global scale. Government budgets are finite and the requirements are many; subsidising bus services, maintaining roads, supporting the arts, education and healthcare responsibilities. These are weighty issues. So it is of vital importance that the decisions taken are done so with a high degree of social responsibility and care. And all of this is set against a backdrop which says 'you won't please all of the people all of the time'. How would you choose between better, more dignified elder care and new books for schools? It is little wonder that decision makers are risk averse in these conditions.

Risk behaviour

Risk is something we are often encouraged to embrace as managers, it is seen as brave and dynamic. It could change the future of the organisation, get us noticed, help us fulfil our ambitions.

However, risk can be dangerous too and there is nothing wrong with managing the business in a steady, measured way. Here are some factors to consider when thinking about your personal attitude to risk.

Desire to do the right thing

Whether through self-preservation, a desire to succeed or a combination of both, most people try hard to do the right thing at work. With risk comes reward, but there is an equal downside if it goes wrong.

Think of this in terms of a new product launch. The reason behind such a strategy would be to increase market share, or break new ground. Here the rewards are clear to see, but what we do know about such innovations is that a high percentage fail (some estimate over 90%). So would you maintain the status quo, carry on farming so to speak, or take a risk on 'death or glory'?

Lack of experience

If you drive a car in an urban environment for the most part, and you occasionally head for open country along narrow lanes, how confident do you feel about overtaking? The reason so many accidents happen during these manoeuvres is the drivers involved have insufficient daily exposure to the technique of safe overtaking, they are poor at judging distance, equally bad at assessing speed of both their own vehicle and others on the road. And their understanding of the limitations of their vehicle is equally flawed.

There are many variable factors to be taken into account, both in the case of the road user and the business manager and, in each instance, if we have had little exposure to the interrelationship between the critical success factors, it comes as no surprise that failure follows.

When so many other factors mitigate against risk taking at work, the chances we get to have a go are strictly limited, so this becomes a self-fulfilling kind of risk apathy. We simply don't feel confident enough to take the chance because we haven't got enough hard data to base our decision upon.

Lack of risk encouragement

If individuals are sometimes afraid of risk, then this is mirrored by organisations. For the reason why, we need only look at what the essence of an organisation is. Beyond the fixed assets, the trading history and the accumulated capital, an organisation is nothing more or less than a collection of individuals who are, at least for the time being, acting as 'key-holders' to the company. Senior managers and CEOs are often only too aware of this, and the weight of responsibility they carry usually means they discourage risk taking amongst their managers.

What is curious is that being slightly 'maverick', 'running close to the wind' is often seen as 'sexy' management, so in order to be perceived as charismatic, senior figures will be heard to encourage risk taking when talking publicly to their staff. The private picture is often much safer.

Inherent danger

'No one ever got fired for buying IBM', that's the legend which has surrounded the company for years. When it was first coined, organisations were only just coming to terms with fax machines, let alone the world of computing (if you are below the age of 25 you may need to look up 'fax machine'!).

Where such uncertainty existed, in what was a market with a lot of hidden pitfalls, IBM capitalised on the fact that they were a known entity, a safe pair of hands. They only needed to hint at the danger of 'going it alone' and nod at the potential repercussions if you as a manager got it wrong.

We all know there are upsides and downsides of risk, but when the punitive measures for making a mistake are spelled out, we might just lower our heads below the parapet for a while.

Evidence from 'history'

Few organisations spring from nowhere to become overnight icons. The dotcom boom of the nineties looked like breaking the old rules, but as is often the way, it eventually came to pass that many of these new start ups, highly valued on the basis of very little trading history or hard evidence, were found to be built on sand. This further reinforced the old adage that 'if it looks too good to be true, it probably is'.

Maybe there is a small part of all us that wants to believe we could make a million from a standing start, if only we had the right idea and fortune smiled upon us. But most of us think it's not likely to happen, simply because 'history dictates'. It looks like there is no easy money out there.

Where the hell have all the leaders gone?

There seems to be more confusion than ever over the management/ leadership debate. Who does which role, what are the levels of responsibility, where does accountability lie?

If there is lack of clarity, risk taking is dangerous. Even the most cavalier of business people will tell you risk should be managed, so if you don't know who is in charge, or responsible for decision making, it is better to stay on the track of safety.

Sometimes the authority that comes with a very senior position can be overwhelming, causing a kind of leadership inertia where the attitude becomes 'what will be, will be'. Under these circumstances, the business carries on doing what it's always done, changing direction or process, procedure or people when forced to do so by outside influences, it becomes wholly reactive.

This contrasts with 'new broom syndrome' which many workers have become tired of, as successive new 'leaders' enter the fray, proclaiming that everything will be better after they've implemented their 'first hundred days' plan.

Risk then is like an unproven myth. Elders tell of its power to change organisations for the better, its recuperative properties are legend, but no one really wants to initialise it.

The combination of personal factors like survival and doing the right thing, allied to organisational imperatives, which take account of the dangers of risk, tend to mean it is the exception, rather than the rule. Rational behaviours tend to take precedence.

The important thing to consider as a manager is whether you lie on the side of rational behaviour or risk behaviour. Circumstances may dictate you lean one way or the other, but only you can judge which is right.

Implementing the right thing in the workplace could be described as rational behaviour as it benefits employees and staff and, if done correctly, will not be to the detriment of the organisation, but it does carry an element of risk, inasmuch as it will require change. As we have seen earlier, this can be difficult to implement and will take skill and good communication.

As Confucius once remarked, 'our greatest honour is not in never failing, but in rising every time we fall'.

Conclusions

Rational behaviour is what keeps many organisations in business

Responsible managers are prepared to do some 'farming'

Risk may appear 'sexy' but it can be dangerous too

Balancing rational and risk behaviours is a matter of personal judgement

CHAPTER 9

The relationship issue

In all our examination of the difficulties of management we have so far carried out, one vitally important element has been missing. The link between practical management tasks and successful outcomes, is the development of good links with staff. How we broker our relationships is the topic we will now look at, before considering the changes we might make. Along the way we will also consider why, for many people, the relationships they make at work are the most significant ones in their lives on a day-to-day basis.

Relationships

Abraham Maslow (1954), had the right idea. In his seminal work on the hierarchy of needs he has 'relationships' at the heart of our wellbeing, right after the food and shelter we all require just to get by. However, does the concept of 'relationships' look any different now, to when he did his work on the subject. Has the nature of how we interact been altered by the society we live in?

Common sense suggests that the constructs of human relationships have changed very little, but because the context has, they're not what they once were. Societal change has meant a diminished reliance on family relationships, due to many factors; rising aspiration has forced many to seek better jobs from further afield, resulting in families being scattered to the four winds. In recessionary times, the imperative may be even greater, as to simply have a job might require a much higher degree of mobility, and a net that needs to be cast further afield. It can be argued that our increased sense of self worth being linked to what we own, has led us to a more selfish, rather than 'selfless' state. Where we once may have felt more tied down by family bonds, now it seems it is okay to 'live our own lives'.

So, if we're no longer as reliant on family ties, what has filled the void? It may be that we just have less relationships, that they're not as close or 'rich' as was once the case, or that the gap has never really been bridged and for many of us, it is a source of unhappiness and our wellbeing is diminished as a result.

What does make sense is for many, the world of work, has become a 'relationship greenhouse', a place where we can substitute some of the familial ties with work-based liaisons.

What makes relationships work?

There are some rare individuals who carry on making friends throughout their entire lives, most of us though form bonds early on, at school, university or in our early careers and tend to rely on these long standing liaisons.

'Relationships' develop through a common sense of values, a shared set of boundaries. Of course, we can have friends who we sometimes violently disagree with, but it is unusual to form a bond with someone if you don't have the same set of shared core values.

As organisations have become more values driven and increasingly self-aware, what they stand for is a large part of what is known as the 'employer brand', that is to say 'the face' the company presents to potential new staff.

The type of organisation we choose and the career path we select, tends to be congruent with our own set of values in that profession. As an example, contrast your opinions of nursing versus investment banking. Neither is necessarily 'better' or 'worse', but their value systems are very different. Consequently, the people who choose each will value different things.

Therefore, in pursuing a particular route, we are likely to encounter co-workers with similar values to our own, so relationships are much more likely to flourish. In a sense, we already have much in common, even before we have even met.

Before we set foot in our workplace, the matches have often been made, simply by dint of the kind of organisation it is.

How relationships form

Long before we get to the stage of sharing more intimate information about our personal values, we begin the process of relationship formation in much safer ground.

In a social situation where adults are being introduced to each other, they will begin the process of building a relationship using two key principles. The first is a 'funnel effect', where at the top is very general, non-threatening information and the further down, the more specific, idiosyncratic and intimate the nature of the revelation. The next principle is about 'reciprocity', so we shall only share the information that is further down in our funnel, the other party is likely to do so too.

Hence, we start at the broad end of the spectrum, typically where people come from, what they do for a living, perhaps how far they travelled to be here. For any kind of bond to form, we have to do one of two things. We either actively look for common ground or we celebrate 'la difference'.

You ask someone where they are from, and begin by trying to make a connection; for example, you used to work in that town, or have friends there, or have visited on a business or social trip. Sometimes the link can be quite tenuous, but remember, we're seeking to bond, so we're trying hard to find the similarities.

Where this can't be done, it is likely that we'll follow up with a supplementary question, which invites the other party to 'fascinate' us, so we say, politely, that we know nothing of their home town, but ask what it's like.

The information we exchange here is important, but often only a part of the picture. Simultaneous to this sharing of facts is a process whereby we are weighing the other person up, in a range of much more sophisticated ways. Mostly we do this unconsciously, but nevertheless form a very fast and surprisingly complete picture.

Let's say, for example, that you have opened the dialogue in the way suggested above, and asked the other party to tell you about their town. Our expectation may be that they give a quick précis of the important points, before pausing to assert their wish for your inclusion, so they'll reciprocate by asking you where you're from. If they go on at length about the history, demographics and current sociological problems without pausing for breath, it won't be long before you have them marked down as a crashing bore.

Similarly, when it comes to the more personal and important topic of values, we are constantly on the look out for hints, signals or indicators that they either share our set, or have a contrary stance. In telling their tale, they are likely to give away their views on important issues, and we form a mental check-list, ticking or crossing against our personal preferences.

Armed with this information, we might be a bit more cautious when seeking to develop some relationships as against others, it will depend on the responses and the accuracy of the match. When we're trying to make a good impression, it's wise to test the water first, to see where the other party is coming from. But under other conditions, maybe on a social basis, you might take the attitude that you don't 'suffer fools gladly', so better to sort out those people who you're likely to get along with, as quickly as possible.

Relationships at work

In the work environment, we tend to form a complex matrix of relationships with those around us. The self awareness tool of 360° feedback has been widely used in management circles (no pun intended) for some time. It seeks to garner opinion from the widest possible range of people we come into contact with, so peers, staff, the boss even our customers are asked to rate us, alongside our own assessment, so that we can compare and contrast what a wide range of different people think.

This disparate collection of individuals will form the core of the relationships we have in the workplace. What we readily recognise is that each will be slightly different from the others; in fact, the hierarchy within work (who reports to whom), begins to determine a parallel hierarchy of relationships, with some being much more significant than others. You don't necessarily have to get along with all your peers, but life will be much harder if you can't form a successful bond with the boss (Robertson and Flint-Taylor 2009).

Most managers and supervisors agonise over the question of how close a relationship they should have with their staff, should you be best friends or keep a professional distance? Here are some contrasting arguments for each.

Best friends

Part of the advantage of forming very close ties with the people who work for us, is that they are likely to place some emotional store by this and work harder, more diligently, honestly and openly with others who form part of the same group. This kind of situation often comes about in small, family run companies, or organisations that have become so large, that they can no longer be defined as a single entity, except in name. This would include something like the National Health Service in the U.K., currently the world's third largest employer. The tendency is for individual teams to see themselves as distinct from the 'corporation'. It's true that people come under the same overarching banner, but staff at the ground level will often feel loyalty to their immediate boss, or at the very most to their department.

While there are many advantages to being 'best friends' for both the individual and the organisation, there are perils too. Managers are often called upon to implement changes that are unlikely to be popular with their staff. At the extreme end of this spectrum is what has euphemistically become called 'down-sizing', otherwise known as 'getting rid of people'!.

There may be compelling business arguments for this course of action, and it is often the cutting of cost by losing *some* people that saves the jobs of the rest. No matter how logical the argument, if you are the one 'for whom the bell tolls', you're unlikely to judge the situation with much objectivity. Instead there will be emotional upset, feelings of rejection and worry over the future. As a 'people manager', this is one of the hardest tasks to perform, both in the decision making phase, and more importantly, during implementation. Imagine then how much more difficult it is likely to be if you were sharing a few drinks with the team on Friday evening, then telling some of them on Monday morning that their services are no longer required.

Professional distance

Because 'best friends' has these distinct disadvantages, many managers like to keep an arms length relationship with their direct reports, but this too has it's difficulties.

If we are to believe the work of Goleman et al (1996), on emotional intelligence, then it follows we need to display many of the behaviours that typify 'making friends', so we know what makes our people tick.

We have already discussed the need for reciprocity in this scenario, so staff members are unlikely to share their hopes, dreams and aspirations, if you remain buttoned up and reticent. Judging just how much to share, becomes a much more difficult task.

Ultimately what often happens in these situations is that we signal quite firmly that there is a limit beyond which we will not go, so the relationship can only develop to a certain point. This can result in our staff seeing us as aloof and elitist, unwilling to be 'one of the gang'. We're grown ups, we can live with that, but it also has an effect on how much co-operation we're likely to get, and how prepared the troops will be to go the extra mile, so necessary in making lots of businesses tick over.

It's interesting to review our relationship-building behaviour in the light of work by Joe Luft and Harry Ingham (1955), who developed the four quadrant Johari Window. This is a model which takes account of what we know of ourselves and what others perceive about us. The significant quadrant according to Luft and Ingham is the 'known' area, where we are self aware about our character and are happy for others to share this knowledge, essentially, we keep little hidden and embrace others with an open spirit.

The level of closeness we have with staff is a personal decision, but try to make it just that, a decision you have consciously taken, not something you have fallen into over time.

Don't forget either that relationships take the co-operation of two parties, and how you get along with others will be governed as much by them as you. Susan Greenfield talked about the uniqueness of human beings, so every encounter is a new challenge. As management thinkers, we spend much of our time trying to categorise people into groups as it makes sense of the world more quickly, so though we recognise uniqueness, here are some types which emerged from recent interviews with managers about their staff.

Moaners, doers, stoics and stars

Moaners – the most difficult people to manage are the ones who find fault with everything. They are just as likely to criticise the status quo as to resist change. From a management perspective moaners sap our energy, not only on their own account, but because if left unchecked, they can have a detrimental effect of the morale of the rest of the team. In the end, their relentlessness can have others believing that they must be right.

Managers report they are often forced to apply the Pareto Principle when dealing with moaners, where 80% of their time is spent on 20% of the staff, which indicates just how difficult it is to deal with this group.

Doers – unquestioning and unambitious, doers simply get on with what they're asked to. All organisations need people like this, simply to keep the 'machine' fed. If they have a weakness, it's that they're not very good with change, preferring to plod along at their own pace, doing what they've always done. However, from a management perspective, they are great people to have in your team. If there is a word of caution it is this, 'don't take doers for granted', or they may just stop doing as efficiently as before.

Stoics – the bounce-back-ability of this type is what sets them apart from many of their colleagues. They tend to be solution-focused, see only the good in those around them and display high degrees of resilience, no matter what is thrown at them.

Stoics often turn out to be the 'secret leaders' in organisations. When your back is turned, and the team are up against it, a stoic will often be the one to pull the others along in their wake. Others often envy them for this. Furthermore, stoics by their nature cope well with change and their natural resilience makes them less prone to stress.

Stars – proactive and high performing, these are the people that drive truly successful organisations. Their tendency towards creativity is an enduring source of competitive advantage in the private sector and the 'can do' stance they take often breaks down the barriers of bureaucracy in the public arena.

Stars are to be cherished and nurtured; they are the leaders of the future. As George Bernard Shaw wrote in Mrs. Warren's Profession, 'people are blaming their circumstances for what they are. I don't believe in circumstances. The people who get on in this world are the people who get up and look for the circumstances they want, and if they can't find them, make them!'

Looking at the relationships we form in the workplace gives us a sense of where we belong, who we are and how others see us. This is a hugely important part of our wellbeing. Looking after this aspect of our lives can be vital in terms of its contribution to our overall happiness.

Viewed in this way, we should not take our relationships in work lightly. Stop and consider for a moment how our behaviour might impact on others, not only in a beneficial sense, but also in potentially damaging the wellbeing of others if we fail to relate in a positive way. This is why we should 'do the right thing'.

Conclusions

As we have become more mobile, our work relationships have assumed greater importance

Forming relationships is a gradual process that demands reciprocity

We need to think carefully and consciously about how close we want to be with our staff

Strong relationships encourage staff to give of their best

CHAPTER 10

Battling the culture

Individual relationships are vitally important in establishing our own part in the organisation, in helping colleagues to cope with the demands upon them, and in contributing to a successful organisation.

Get a group of individuals together though, and before you know it, you will have created an organisational culture. A hard-to-define corporate 'personality', which all those involved readily recognise, but are not able to pinpoint its origins or how it grew so big and immutable! So, what's wrong with culture? The answer is very little, it can be a huge benefit to organisations as it performs the function of providing a shorthand for expected behaviours. Its only slight drawback, is when you are considering change, (as in moving towards a set of new wellbeing behaviours). Cultures, the unwritten rules, often stand in the way.

Michael Angus, once chairman of Unilever, described culture as 'what people do when they're not thinking about it'. Indeed, it is notoriously hard to describe and yet everyone seems to fall in behind a culture, knowing instinctively how to behave in a congruent way.

If you have worked in a number of different organisations, you will know the way each operates can be very different, yet our ability to adapt, so we fit in, is usually highly developed. Individuals who join an organisation and are counter-cultural in a big way, tend not to last, either because they break the rules and are dismissed, or feel they are banging their heads against the proverbial brick wall and ultimately give up the fight themselves.

Elements of culture

Some behavioural aspects can help us to get a stronger defin-ition of what culture is about, as we can start to contrast them from one organisation to another. By examining the component parts, we begin to get a sense of what culture is. Types of behav-iour are discussed below, with examples of where they are most likely to exist, and some analysis of the benefits or pitfalls of each. Consider where your current organisation lies with regard to these cultural traits.

Politeness is a good starting point. The degree to which col-leagues are prepared to help each other, goes hand-in-hand with this. High levels of politeness tend to be found in service sectors, which have a lot of transactional dealings with cus-tomers, particularly if these are face-to-face. The retail sector is a good example. It's not that behind the scenes there is 'one big happy family', of course there are disputes between colleagues and people fall out, but the continual professional demand on workers to be polite to customers does tend to rub off in their dealings with each other.

This provides us with a heartening lesson, inasmuch as behav-iours can create their own momentum if they are displayed often enough, by sufficient numbers of workers on a consistent basis. We will return to this theme later when we look at creating a cultural shift.

Politeness can go a long way towards creating a harmonious workplace in some situations, but it can be perceived as a sign of weakness. There is a feeling in this context that underperformance can sometimes be ignored, or not addressed with sufficient rigour as managers are 'too polite' to take this on. So politeness should not be championed as 'a place to hide', but rather as a way of creating and sustaining less stressful work relationships.

At the opposite end of the spectrum is aggression, sometimes prevalent in organisations where tasks are mission critical, for example, in the military. A degree of controlled aggression is sometimes necessary to carry out duties. This can then spill over into the day-to-day dealings of the organisation, even when it's not involved in a conflict situation. Organisations with a high profit drive can also suffer from aggression, as those at the sharp end battle it out with competitors, or sometimes with their own colleagues.

Aggressive organisations would claim the benefit of their culture is directness, to the point where everyone knows exactly where they stand and as a consequence of this there is no time wasted on 'niceties'. It is plain to see in this environment, stress levels are likely to be high. Furthermore, periods of tenure can be short, especially in the pressure cooker of financial trading, where people are frequently seen to 'burn out'.

Respect is a related behaviour, but a good measure in its own right. Hierarchical companies, with rigid structures and strong performance management, tend to perpetuate a culture of respect, at least on the surface. Here you would not expect to see any open criticism of management. Contrast this with creative or vocational organisations, where the 'freedom of speech' culture often allows for a flagrant disregard for the sensibilities of managers. Many large public sector organisations fall into this category, caught between operational complexities and the need to save money, managers are often seen as 'getting in the way', and a disrespectful culture ensues.

Laurence – Admin assistant

'I couldn't believe it when I started work at my local council, people openly criticised the managers, sometimes even in front of them. If anything bad had happened locally and the press got hold of it, you'd see the article pinned up on notice boards the next day, as if to prove how hopeless our leaders were.

That would never have happened when I worked in private companies. Of course people would have a good whinge about the boss, who doesn't from time to time, but it was all in hushed tones during the coffee break'.

While 'freedom of speech' is a desirable element of an open culture, it is not helpful if all the speech is negative. As President Reagan once said, 'I've always believed that a lot of the trouble in the world would disappear if we were talking to each other instead of about each other'.

Finally, there is the aspect of culture which is to do with personal initiative. This defines the level of freedom employees have to fulfil their role in the best way they think fit. Encouraging staff to problem-solve for themselves is a good way of building satisfaction into the role, rather than a process of spoon-feeding which allows for little initiative.

Managers in these organisations need to accept they will have less control, as each staff member may approach a task in a different way, but the corresponding 'up side' of this approach is a greater level of engagement and the increased likelihood of 'discretionary behaviour', where employees are prepared to 'go the extra mile'.

How can we change the culture?

Don't underestimate the challenge. As Machiavelli wrote in *The Prince*, 'It should be borne in mind that there is nothing more difficult to arrange, more doubtful of success and more dangerous to carry through than initiating change…The innovator makes enemies of all those who prospered under the old order, and only lukewarm support is forthcoming from those who would prosper under the new'.

It would be naïve to believe that dramatic shifts in culture are easy to bring about, but a gradual shift *is* possible if we get to the core of the issue. In a sense, the established culture of an organisation can be likened to a kind of mass hysteria, enough people displaying the same behaviours, with the individual joining the crowd or becoming overwhelmed.

However, in very large organisations we often find the presence of micro cultures, whose behaviours don't *exactly* match the greater mass of employees. Often it is individual managers who at the heart of this phenomenon, interpreting the bigger picture in a way which makes sense for their own team, and ignoring some of the initiatives that don't match up with the overall value system.

To mitigate against the mass hysteria of the rest of the organisation, takes courage and self belief, but here is a suggested four point plan which may help in the way you think about the changes ahead.

Before embarking upon it, it is helpful to have a 'mission ethos', a reason for attempting this difficult and perhaps thankless task. We could call this 'a culture of one, based on the right thing'. This is a commitment to yourself which says you are no longer prepared to simply fit in, if what you are fitting in with is wrong, in future you are going to do the right thing come hell or high water. This is not as anarchic as it sounds. Many managers 'lose their way' in organisations and when asked to indulge in deep personal reflection are uneasy with how they have compromised their principles to fit in with the culture.

Four steps to cultural change

1. Start swimming – people are often quite good at defining the culture of their organisation, provide them with a flip chart and they'll come up with a range of adjectives which accurately sum up the 'personality' of their enterprise. What none of us seem to be so good at is identifying who began the culture or how it is perpetuated. The plain truth is that for most, culture is not so much a movement in one direction, as an inertia which results in us getting swept along with the tide.

If we stop bobbing about and begin to move our arms and legs a little, we might begin to have some influence over the direction of travel. This is harder work than simply going with the flow, but our sense of purpose is underpinned by a desire to make the future better.

Turning through 180° and swimming headlong into the advancing tide, might be too much effort all at once, and we'd end up being overwhelmed. Better then to find a 'tangent of least resistance', and swim at an angle to the established flow, turning more into the masses as our 'campaign' gathers weight.

2. In order to increase the momentum of your change, it's a good idea to bring some fellow travellers along in your slipstream. If your team are faithful supporters and really desire a 'better' workplace, they will readily join your campaign. Be sure to let them know in advance that the journey will be a tougher one than if they carry on bobbing along with the masses. Equally, you will need to keep reminding your posse of the progress you have made, or they may be inclined to give up. Set yourself some short term achievable goals, and proclaim these quick wins as they occur in order to keep motivation high.

3. Encourage those in your 'right thing' movement to recruit others by buddying up with every passing worker. Your objective is to form a shoal, a significant body of 'rightness' moving as one, at an angle to the mob. This should be sufficient for them to notice you are different, but not so much they feel intimidated by it. As we have said, you can turn more into the tide as time goes by and your momentum and strength increase. For now concentrate on increasing the numbers until you form a side culture, one which isn't incongruent with what's gone before, but eradicates any negative elements which may have damaged wellbeing, like for example, an embedded long working hours culture.

4. Wait for the tide to turn. Eventually, with enough people on your side, the old regime will begin to be forgotten. The 'bobbers', those who were inclined to be simply dragged along with the masses, will now start to be pulled in a different direction, a more positive one, and soon they will hardly notice the difference. Except the future will be different, because it will have been shaped by your actions, and determination to see the right thing implemented for the good of everyone.

The result of all this hard work will sometimes be difficult to see because the journey is a long one and a struggle. However, with perseverance you will eventually reap what you sow and will end up working in an environment more conducive to your own view of the world. One which is better for your wellbeing and those around you.

Conclusions

Culture is often hard to define, but it can be explained by behaviours

Many are swept up in organisational culture, simply through apathy

Changing culture is a long game, so be prepared

Good leadership is needed to help people through

The benefits of positive culture change are worth the effort in delivering wellbeing

CHAPTER 11

Three cases for change

For all our analysis to this point of the difficulties of the work-place, and the significance of our relationships and culture, we would not wish to forward the argument that the modern world of work is broken beyond repair. However, it is in the nature of management and leadership thinking that we strive for continuous improvement, not only in terms of system and process efficiency, but also, more importantly, in the way we treat people.

There is often no good reason to maintain a state which is quite obviously flawed and yet we do. This premise is central to the theme of the book *Nudge*, by Richard Thaler and Cass Sunstein who present excellent arguments for why we should be 'persuaded' to change our behaviour, for our own good. Take their example of pension plans. Saving for old age is logical. We all assume we will reach an age where we will want to enjoy our retirement in relative comfort. And yet, the evidence shows, even when presented with the facts about the finances, not nearly enough people begin to make provision for their old age in time. Thaler and Sunstein believe we should be nudged into doing the right thing for our own benefit.

So what is it that has stopped us implementing 'right thing' policies in the workplace so far?

History

'This is the way we've always done things around here', the clarion call of older workers in the organisation, who after many years of service, believe that they know best. Senior physician,

Sir George Alberti talks of how the naysayers in the NHS will say 'we tried doing it that way in 1974 and it didn't work'. He goes on to make the point that the suggested change may well have not worked in the past, but since then, the world has moved, on and maybe it's time to think about how this particular strategy fits into a modern context.

Incentive

There are limits to our written and psychological contracts with an employer. We don't sell our soul when we join. So too, there are limits on how far we are prepared to go to achieve the 'excellent service' or 'return on investment', the things which are part of the staged objectives of the enterprise. Mostly, we will do our jobs to the best of our ability, based on the incentive the employer offers, what reason is there for going beyond this? Change can be painful, so there are few of us who will vote for more of it, especially if this risks our own future or that of our close colleagues.

Status quo

The level of emotional involvement with the firm has its limits too, and for workers who are on top of their jobs, the office can be a cosy place, where aside from the occasional hassle, things tick along quite nicely for most of the time. Even if, deep down, we are aware that the company is not doing the right thing, it might feel okay; it may be a case of 'better the devil you know...'

Fear of the unknown

The managers who implement change on a minute-by-minute basis in organisations are often the very same people who are most resistant to alterations in their own operations. So we may deride the dinosaurs who don't want to move forward, but are we just like them? Fear of change might be based on 'hard won experience' from the past. Losing our job in a round of redundancies is something we are neither likely to forget, or want to repeat, so our fears may be well founded.

But whatever resistance you see around you, or feel from within, the arguments in favour of change are strong. Let's begin by looking at what the science says.

The scientific case

Earlier we discussed the issue of stress in the workplace, and the damaging effect this has on individuals, co-workers and the friends and families of those afflicted by it (Lundberg and Cooper 2010).

Wellbeing, the positive state of having a healthy body and mind, a state that can be said to be one notch down from happiness and fulfilment, is more than an *absence* of stress. There are positive elements to wellbeing which we can and will promote, but at the same time, it is also true that the opposite end of the spectrum of 'wellness' is populated by anxiety, depression and stress (these common mental disorders are prevalent in 1 in 5 of the population in the U.K. and many other countries in the world).

It is fair to argue that removing or reducing stress represents a huge stride forward in the direction of well being. So, what are the trigger points of stress in the workplace, and will doing the right thing help to mitigate against them? The following reasons are culled from interviews with workers who claim to have felt workplace stress.

Uneven workload – the workflow varies with 'pinch points', where everything is needed at once, followed by periods of boredom. Often the unpredictability of the flow of work was cited as part of the problem, preventing workers from 'gearing up' for the busy spells.

Lack of parity or fairness – sometimes referred to as 'teacher's pet' syndrome, where a colleague of the same grade is looked upon more favourably. This is played out in terms of the tasks allocated (the 'pet' always gets the plum jobs), time off, financial incentive, performance management and promotion. A sense of injustice sometimes led to very deep seated resentment and high levels of tension.

Tight deadlines – workers often recognised the need for tight deadlines, and reported that on a one-off basis they were fine. When one followed another with no respite between, stress levels or the perception of stress rose. Often the requirement to hit deadlines was linked to lack of parity (see earlier), with favoured co-workers not being called upon to complete tasks in the same time frame.

Unrealistic expectations – a sense of 'however good we are, it's never enough' was evidenced by increases in expectation year on year. This was commonplace in sales roles, where whatever the level of previous success might have been, there was an expectation more could be delivered. Processes with measurable outputs, like in manufacturing, suffered the same fate.

Aggressive or un-co-operative colleagues – one of the causes of the highest stress levels was the breakdown in relationships between workers. This was often cited as a 'stress without boundaries', both in terms of how acute it could become and, tellingly, in that it was not restricted to the physical space of the workplace, many took this kind of stress home with them, talking of disrupted sleep and anxiety.

A bullying boss – workers felt an utter hopelessness when faced with a boss who bullied them. For many, they were faced with an uncomfortable choice between resigning their post or tolerating the current situation. Often, they claimed it was the 'not knowing what to expect' which was most stressful, beginning each day unsure of whether it would be calm or confrontational.

New tasks – growth-in-job can be one of the most satisfying workplace experiences, but it is not always stress free. Some interviewees reported a growing sense of panic over not being able to complete a new task to the required standard or timescale.

In our earlier chapter on stress, we calibrated some of the costs of stress, and these in themselves go a long way to building a scientific case for change. But there is more if we project forward into the future. If stress levels continue to increase in the workplace and go unaddressed, what will be the state of our corporations in ten years time?

And the costs we incur are not simply a matter of calculating sickness absence and measuring the number of lost days. The implications for the wider community are potentially highly damaging.

Stress is, in a sense, infectious, inasmuch as when someone close has it, we very often feel a milder form too. The burden for families could extend into a growing weight of pressure on the entire health system.

Because stress comes in many forms and at differing levels of severity, workers often fail to report or acknowledge it and often learn to deal with the symptoms. The danger here is that managers can become tempted to ignore the problem, reasoning that it will go away of its own accord. The scientific evidence shows this is often not the case.

The organisational case

We examined the costs of stress to organisations earlier, and in economic terms they are vast. In fact, one of the difficult issues is to find a methodology which can accurately track these costs, as the complex matrix of repercussions of stress lead us down so many different alleys. It is perhaps more beneficial to consider on an individual basis the cost to each company, estimated across a range of factors identified by Robertson and Cooper (2011), When you have read through the list, consider the implications of *not* following a programme which promotes better wellbeing, and you will have uncovered much of the organisational case. Put simply, can any organisation afford to ignore the wellbeing of their workforce?

• Sick leave
• Early retirement

- Replacement costs associated with employee turnover (recruitment, training and development)
- Grievances, disputes and compensation
- Damage to equipment and decreased productivity due to accidents/errors
- Decreased performance and productivity
- Loss of company reputation

In tandem with the studies which have chartered the rise in stress at work, (Lundberg and Cooper 2010), much has been done to try and understand the factors which may bring about better wellbeing.

There is now evidence to show a positive correlation between well being and productivity (Donald et al 2005; Cropanzano and Wright 2007). Furthermore as the performance curve rises in line with increased wellbeing, this in itself leads to workers feeling better. A virtuous cycle is created.

As well as being good for society and the individuals affected, the truth is 'happy workers are productive workers' (Hosie and Cooper 2006). But what exactly do we mean by 'happiness' and 'productivity' in this instance?

To add some depth to the definitions, here is a list of human statements about happiness at work:

'I feel much better now I get home in time to see the kids'

'My boss is great, she tells me what needs doing without shouting all the while'

'I make up the time if I need to leave early for family reasons'

'It feels like the work is shared out evenly between us'

'My colleagues help me out when I am struggling'

'It's comforting to know that I can get out of work if there's a crisis at home'

'For me, work is work and home is home, they don't interfere with each other'

'I like my job, it's not just a way of paying the bills'

'Not everything I do is interesting, but overall the balance is pretty good'

'I like being with people, I feel like I'm part of a team'

Such statements begin to build a pattern of what makes workers happy with their jobs. The main themes that emerge are as follows;

1. I have some control over my working life, although the expectations are high in terms of output and accuracy, if I need time off for any reason, the process is quite simple. I don't take advantage of this, as I consider it a valuable privilege

2. The quality of the tasks I do is important. I don't expect every aspect of my working life to be thrilling, but would be very de-motivated if it was all dull. Having a balance of things to do means I'm never far away from a task I like

3. Inclusion is important to me; I like to feel that I'm part of something. I am definitely more prepared to put myself out for one of my co-workers if they're having a bad time, because I know that they would do the same for me. I am always keen to let them know this, so they too feel supported

4. The atmosphere at work is good, I never witness any bullying. We can all feel the pressure sometimes, particularly when there is a tight deadline, but this doesn't spill over into the way we treat each other. If anything it makes us more focused on the task and more determined to achieve it together

We can now repeat this exercise but instead of focusing on happiness, let us look at productivity.

'It feels like we get through more when we work as a team'

'I work harder now, though I get less stressed, I think it's because I feel supported'

'In the last 6 months we've achieved much more than I'd expected'

'Work hard, play hard, that's our motto'

'Our boss is happy to trust us to get on with our jobs'

'Often we get praise from customers and it feels good'

'I find I can switch off at home if I've had a hard day at work'

The main productivity themes are as follows:

1. We're not afraid of hard work; in fact we thrive on it, as long as the whole team is in it together. Our collective sense of achievement is what motivates us to do even better next time

2. Mutual support and trust is a big part of what keeps us going. Even when we have tough deadlines to meet the sense of camaraderie is strong enough to keep us going

3. We're managed with a light touch. The tasks and the road ahead are set for us, then it's our responsibility to deliver what is asked for

These collected statements about the level of contentment workers feel or the attitude they have to their roles are exactly what managers want to hear. It reflects a highly motivated, self-starting team with a genuine interest in doing the job to the best of their ability. The support strategies they have put in place help to dilute the stress of pressurised situations, and the healthy balance in their lives, keeps them mentally and physically fit for their jobs.

The final piece of the 'organisational case' jigsaw comes in the form of corporate social responsibility, alluded to in our examination of stress. Beyond the profit ethic of many commercial enterprises, there has been a significant shift towards sustainability. This covers a multitude of issues, from responsible sourcing, through care over the carbon footprint, right down to how we treat our people.

Any organisation which claims in its value statement to advocate CSR, must therefore embrace a policy which looks out for the financial, physical and mental welfare, of their staff.

These factors in themselves are usually sufficient to convince any boss about the organisational case for change, but add them to the scientific case, where the number of lost days through stress can be reduced, and the case is inarguable.

The emotional case

When we stray from logic and statistical data, it's much harder to compile a robust case for better wellbeing, so a leap of faith is required when we say to businesses that they should 'do the right thing', simply because it is the right thing.

Consider the family values we were raised with, like care and consideration for others, kindness, community spirit, integrity and honesty. With imagination and insight, it is possible to come up with measures of goodness, but measurement aside, if they are as we suggest intrinsically good, both for us and society as a whole, shouldn't we just embrace them anyway, without the need for 'proof'?

Our emotional ties, and relationships with those closest to us in life, should also demand that we maximise our wellbeing at work, so we are fully emotionally functioning at home. Even more important is the need to keep the two states in kilter, so that we divide our time between our jobs and our homes in a way that delivers us a lifestyle of 'maximum affluence without emotional starvation'.

So, our time commitment to the workplace can be said to be limited by the plateau of our financial ambitions (we can always spend more), to the point where it is not damaging the relationships we have at home. Every pound or dollar over this level, risks increasing our financial worth *to the detriment* of our emotional wellbeing (and that of our loved ones).

Camille

'I worked for a big investment bank in the City. I earned a lot of money, I mean a lot. But that means you have to put in the hours, it's gone beyond the point where it's just kind of expected, it's compulsory (not written down of course, but those who don't do it, don't last).

I had a colleague whose kids were similar ages to mine, 8 and 6, and very occasionally we'd swap stories about them, not that we had much to say, as they'd all been brought up by Nannies and Au Pairs from an early age.

Maybe I just picked up the air of sadness about her, but in the end I quit my job and went to become a full time mum. I'm not taking the moral high ground, it was simply that she made me see what was important in my life, it was the right thing for me'.

It is not unusual for working parents (mothers in particular), to have misgivings over whether they are making the right choices. The guilt associated with spending too little family time is rarely compensated for by the additional disposable income. Even if we have no children, the emotional ties we have are no less significant. We need to make time for our families and friends.

For a majority of us in adult life, a partner, wife or husband is the most important individual relationship we have. The evidence is now pointing to a 'stress transfer phenomenon', where even if we return home chilled out and relaxed, we can 'inherit' the tension of our stressed out partner, despite not having witnessed the cause of their stress at first hand.

Doing the right thing is clear in these conditions, we owe it to someone we love, not to do this to them.

The three case rationale for change may have convinced you that some action needs to be taken, both for the sake of your own wellbeing and those within your sphere of influence at work, which might include your staff, peers, boss and the wider community of colleagues, customers and suppliers you encounter.

In the coming chapters we will examine how to implement a series of regular new behaviours, which have been shown to increase wellbeing in the long term.

Conclusions

Scientific evidence is beginning to show the cost of lost days due to a lack of wellbeing

There is direct positive link between happy workers and productivity

Our out-of-work relationships provide a good rationale for maximising our wellbeing

The overall weight of evidence points towards a need to proactively embrace wellbeing

CHAPTER 12

Setting incremental goals

When we discussed the nature of change in the workplace, we used the analogy of watching children grow. It happens so gradually that on a daily basis no one notices, it's only in retrospect that we realise just how radical the change has been.

Similarly, if you decide you are going to begin to change things at work, and adopt some new behaviours, it's a good idea to implement this a little at a time, if you are going to avoid startling your colleagues.

This will also reduce the risk of failure, as each incremental change you make can be allowed time to bed in and become the norm, before moving on to the next. The ideal scenario is to build small changes, one at a time, on top of each other, although hardly noticeable at first, they soon begin to make a substantial difference.

If you think back to your personal experience of making New Year's resolutions, you may have had times when you have attempted to change on every front; lose weight, get fit, quit smoking etc., a very long list. This make it much more likely you will fail at all of these than if you concentrate on one small change at a time.

Sometimes being 'evangelical' about our intended actions can bring other people on side, at others it can turn them off, so only you can judge this. Perhaps a good halfway house is to have a 'change confidante', a trusted friend or colleague who you can outline your ideas and intent to, who will support you quietly from the sidelines and who will provide a listening ear, if, or when things don't match up to your expectations.

This kind of mentoring can be hugely beneficial, as we sometimes need to be told we're doing the right thing, to reinforce the courage of our convictions. It is not necessarily the case that your confidante needs to be someone you work with. If they do, they will more readily understand your issues, but if not, they have the benefit of external objectivity which can be a huge asset when seeking a sense of proportion.

Further advice is to 'choose changes that are actually possible'. This means considering if they are within your field of influence and authority, and consistent with the aims of the organisation you work for.

We have talked extensively about organisational culture, and it is this factor above all others, which defines behaviours in the workplace. As we are part of the culture, we have not only the right to begin changing it, but also the *responsibility* to.

Knowing what you are attempting is a 'just cause' should help strengthen your resolve, your determination and self confidence, which is going to be necessary when you come up against resistance.

All of the suggested changes we talk about are covered under the banner of 'behaviour', although you may feel that it is process and procedures which need an overhaul at your workplace. The truth is that there are many different ways of carrying out process and over time, if the behaviours are right, you will optimise the methods.

In discussion groups with managers, we often observed widely differing opinions of 'what was allowed' in the organisation. At the 'risk averse' end of the scale, there were some who could cite different items of policy and procedure, quote verbatim from compliance orders and point you to the bit on the intranet that outlined all the rules. Their polar opposites, at the 'maverick' end of the scale, would simply shrug and say they had been doing what they thought was right for years, irrespective of what the rule book said, and no one had stopped them yet.

This is not leading to advice which suggests you flout the rules at every turn, but instead to reflect on the fact that there is often a different way of *interpreting* the rules. The 'mavericks' operate on the basis that it is better to ask forgiveness than permission. These discussions often proved uncomfortable for all concerned. The group who didn't like risk felt uneasy that some of their colleagues were not 'compliant', and the ones who had been 'getting away with it' didn't want their issues raised publicly, in case they were forced to ask if it was okay to operate this way, with the inevitable conclusion that the answer would be 'no'.

We found that the complexity of these situations was magnified in organisations where lots of merger and takeover had happened, (Finkelstein and Cooper 2010), or in public sector bodies that had come together under a common banner. This is consistent with the fact that micro-cultures had existed in each component part, in the days when they were separate. Sometimes it takes a very long time for the cultures to merge into one. The important point to note is, largely speaking, the organisation continues to function, albeit with the odd altercation here and there.

Setting a philosophy for incremental change

We live in a target driven world. At work we are set annual objectives in line with organisational strategy, our performance is monitored, our success measured. In private life the targeting is more subtle, less formal, but peer and family pressures, media influence and our own ambition, often coalesce into a set of aspirations we have for ourselves and our futures.

One of the most annoying aspects of this process is its never-ending nature. We hit a target another is set, we achieve a personal goal and another looms large. To overcome this, means we have to stop seeing a fixed process before us where the end is in sight. Without being too morbid, the only real end is when we cease to be, but long before that we should see our achievements for what they are, and feel proud of them, whether it's a certain status within the firm, being thought of as a good parent or partner or overcoming some adversity that has blocked our way. As Studs Terkel wrote in his acclaimed book, *Working*, 'work should be about a search for daily meaning as well as daily bread, for recognition as well as cash, for astonishment rather than torpor, in short for a sort of life rather than a Monday through Friday sort of dying'.

The question is an old one, is the glass half full or half empty? So do we feel great about all the good things we have already done, or frustrated that there is still so much to do? For the sake of our sanity and happiness, it's good to take a balanced approach. We should surely have a sense of achievement about our past successes, safe in the knowledge of, but undaunted by, the challenges which lie ahead.

Goal setting – handle with care

'Objectives should be SMART', this is the advice we are given during our school days and onwards at every training course we ever attend. In the unlikely event that you have avoided this mnemonic so far, it stands for specific, measurable, achievable, realistic and time-bound.

In a general sense, it is not a bad thing, but beware of being wedded to it. There is an obvious early pitfall, which is the drawing of a distinction between 'realistic' and 'achievable. Often they mean the same thing. The SMART formula also has a tendency to fall down when it is applied to creative pursuits. For example, how do you set a meaningful target for playing the piano, or learning to paint? What level of skill constitutes success? Maybe even Eric Clapton has his own guitar heroes?

We have acknowledged that with change in the workplace or bringing up children, the improvements and alterations we make are barely discernable at the time. However, when we look back over some time and distance, we are able to recognise the great strides we have made. A common illustration of this is people in their middle to later years saying 'if I'd known back then what I know now'. Whatever aspect of their knowledge they're talking about, it wasn't magically acquired when they awoke one day, it was hard won, incrementally, over a long period.

This means having an ambition to set objectives which take us closer to the right thing, and improve the wellbeing of ourselves and those around us, is not so much about using SMART against a fixed end point, but much more to do with an ethos which says 'a little better each day' and we could add 'in perpetuity'.

This philosophy borrows heavily from the Japanese principle of Kaizen, popularised in manufacturing companies after World War 2. Introduced into Japan by American management experts, the method, which relies on a great attention to detail and a relentless pursuit of 'better', was instrumental in the recovery of both individual companies and the manufacturing economy as a whole.

The convenient truth of this ethos is it is unlikely to ruffle any feathers at work, because even for those who are involved with the process of change, they may hardly notice it's happening, until it already has.

Measurement by reflection

Those of us used to gauging our success based on hard measures, may at first be uncomfortable with something as nebulous as this. We may be naturally drawn to the question of measurement. How will we calibrate the improvements we seek to make?

Once again, we need to throw convention to the wind, firstly, by setting timescales that are beyond the 12 months of the performance review cycle, and secondly, by utilising our reflective skills.

The thing which most often stops us from doing this, is finding the time. The process is simplicity itself. Once you have determined the frequency of your reflections, you need to consider three aspects.

a. What was the journey (where were we before and what milestones did we pass to get here)?
b. Where are we now (and how does it differ from the old state)?
c. How did this happen?

Because our memories can play tricks on us, especially in the long term, it is worth keeping a written log of these musings, in order to capture the learning effectively.

The purpose of monitoring in this way, beyond simply telling us where we're up to, is to act as a positive motivational force to drive us on. If we're surrounded by negative workers who think 'nothing ever gets better around here', we will need some evidence to show it does.

The success of your 'right thing' campaign might be a cause for solitary celebration. If you are on a lonely crusade towards improvement, you will need all the encouragement you can get, even if it's provided by your own reflective log.

We have talked in some detail about incremental change, sustained over time, about the concept of Kaizen, 'a little better each day', so don't feel daunted that you have to heal everyone's world overnight and turn them into deliriously happy people, take it slowly.

But where to start?

Coming up, we will examine the foundations of wellbeing in terms of five commonly recognised behaviours which are based on current research. We will then look at how we can adapt and adopt this learning for the workplace by looking at the physical space of where we work (which we call environomics), the time we devote to our organisation (harmonisation) and the relationships we form in the process (embrace).

Conclusions

Big changes happen over time, set small, regular goals to get there

You are taking on organisational culture, it won't all change overnight

Don't be deterred by a lack of hard measures, use 'reflection' to gauge your success

Reflect on your success; use this to bolster your efforts in the future

CHAPTER 13

Five new behaviours

There are a growing number of studies into wellbeing (Robertson and Cooper 2011), which are beginning to coalesce into a set of behaviours which the evidence shows are good for us.

Some of these have been known about for a while, others may seem obvious but the work of the U.K. Government's Foresight project (Cooper et al 2009), brought many of the most significant research studies together and examined the evidence, resulting in recommendations on behaviour.

The study, which was published in 2008, aimed to examine the state of the nation's mental capital and wellbeing, in order to establish what challenges we would face in the coming years in relation to these issues. Over a thousand pages of analysis followed, with rigorous evidence-based conclusions and thoughtful speculation about the changing nature of the world we live in.

In recognition of the fact this might have limited use to the average hard-pressed individual, the final conclusions section of the study narrows down the research to five behaviours, which we outline below.

Further work has since been done to flesh out the behaviours and make them understandable through practical examples of how they might be achieved. The New Economics Foundation (www.neweconomics.org), have been responsible for some of this work, and both the findings of the original study and their further interpretation are to be found in the public domain across a range of media. NHS hospital trust websites (www.solihullnhs.uk), have carried the précis of '5 ways to wellbeing' and national newspapers, such as *The Guardian* (Society Guardian, 06.04.2011), have similarly used the findings as part of wider reports on health and wellbeing.

For our part, the challenge has been to consider the practicalities of these recommendations, and to find ways of applying them not only in day-to-day interactions, but more significantly in the workplace, so that we might improve our own wellbeing and keep a watchful eye on the 'health' of our staff.

Following an examination of the behaviours, we will move on to look at how they can be translated and applied in work situations. There is no proscribed timescale or frequency for each behaviour. However, just as we might try to ensure we eat five portions of fruit and vegetables a day for the sake of our diet, if we similarly try to exercise all these behaviours per day, the overall effect on our wellbeing should be significant.

Here are the conclusions of the research, summed up in the five behaviours discussed.

1. Connect

Proactively be a part of society. The way we live today means we can easily become isolated. For many, we no longer have family nearby, we may be working long hours and have little social time. We might not have a social network in the workplace. Under these circumstances it is easy to fall into a pattern of work, followed by evenings spent alone, only to face the same the next day. Weekends can degenerate into solo activity with little outside stimulus. Many old people who have difficulty getting out begin to feel a similar sense of isolation.

In order to overcome this, we need to be proactive in our connections, rather than await a knock on the door or the phone to ring. The curious thing about so-called social media, is that it can increase isolation. Online many individuals report having hundreds of friends, but the reality is they only exist in a virtual sense in cyberspace. Connections need to include face-to-face interaction for some of the time.

For outgoing gregarious types this activity is easy, but not everyone is so ready to start chatting to strangers. Connecting can be much simpler than this though, looking for opportunities to smile, make eye contact or simply say hello is a good enough starting point.

In a supermarket environment, helping someone reach an item from a high shelf or alternatively, asking for help yourself is a simple connection. Often, just being willing to listen to others will begin the process.

William

'I guess I'm like most people, always in a rush, never enough time to fit everything in. So one day, I'm helping my daughter with her paper round when an old guy comes out of his house and engages me in conversation. Like lots of folks his age, he just wants to reminisce about his days in the army. After a couple of minutes I'm shifting from foot to foot and looking at my watch. After ten minutes I'm sitting with him on a bench in front of his house, rapt with attention. He shows me the shrapnel scar on his scalp, tells me how he walked across continents, survived the attention of wolves and other predators, he turns out to be fascinating. At 86 years of age, I wonder how many more times he'll get to tell those great stories, and the paper round pales into insignificance. Now I give his door a knock every couple of weeks, just to see how he is and keep an eye on him.'

Connections can start with the simplest of things, but we need to be prepared to make the first move. When we're hard pressed for time we might be inclined to 'walk on by', but try to remember both parties benefit from making a connection. They are an excellent way of helping us get a sense of perspective over what is really important in our lives.

In the workplace, we are often limited by our roles and may have little understanding of what other departments do. Making connections by chatting in the lift or at the queue of the staff restaurant can give us a much broader view of the whole picture. It is also a fantastic way to network and encouraged inter-departmental collaboration.

2. Take notice

Although we are only looking at the second element of the 5 behaviours, the first thing that begins to strike us is the inter-connection between each of the recommendations. 'Taking notice of other people around us' will help when we are think-ing about making connections, like the story William told. However there is more to it than this. Taking notice means of everything. Beyond observing the world around us, the beauty of nature, the first flowers of spring, it is almost a personal philosophy of 'awareness'.

Taking notice can be the feeling of exhilaration we get, driving an open top car on a sunny day down a deserted road, but the memory of it is not enough, the awareness at the time is the critical element, it is about living in the now.

Too often we live our lives through reminiscences of the past or in planning the future, promising ourselves that everything will be alright when...well, whenever. How often do we allow our-selves the luxury of stopping and thinking that this moment right now is a great one?

People in their forties and fifties think back fondly to their youth, the lack of responsibility they had then, good looks, fitness, excellent health, but people in their seventies and eight-ies yearn to be 40 or 50 again, no aches and pains, old enough to have some experience and wisdom, young enough to know what to do with it. There is goodness in every stage of our lives, if only we can seek it out.

According to author and US National Memory Champion Joshua Foer (Guardian Newspaper, 09.04.2011), our ability to develop our intelligence can be enhanced by a greater awareness of what is going on around us, 'what I had really trained my brain to do, as much as to memorise, was to be more mindful and to pay attention to the world around me. Remembering can only happen if you decide to take notice'.

The more we give ourselves time in a conscious way to take notice, the more it will begin to happen of its own accord. This is a good habit to form; it helps you understand your place in the world, particularly in the context of the people you work with day in and day out.

3. Be active

The links between good physical fitness and mental wellbeing are well established, not only due to the endorphin release we get from vigorous exercise, but also because of the buzz we feel from looking after ourselves. Over time we create a virtuous circle of improvement, the better we look and feel, the more we want to keep that way.

It's not about setting a target to run a marathon, but more to do with choosing activity that you enjoy and look forward to. Some people are happy with solo pursuits like road running, for them it is a challenge to match or beat their previous times, or run for longer. And because no one else is involved, there is freedom of choice when to do it. For others, competitive sport against an opponent or being part of a team is more enjoyable, with the obvious benefit of a social side to the activity.

Whatever you choose, the important factor is to keep exercising regularly in order to maximise the benefit. Having some kind of planned schedule will help with this.

Once more, the links with other behaviours are plain to see, if part of your exercise regime is to go for a brisk walk, it would be difficult not to 'take notice' along the way, so you are completing two of your five behaviours in one go. Bump into a fellow walker en route and you've added 'connect' to your list!

4. Keep learning

Enduring curiosity is part of keeping mentally fit. After years in full time education, many of us turn our backs on the classroom and stop making deliberate forays into formal learning. It doesn't have to be this way, not if we are learning something we enjoy. Often practical skills get ignored in the school curriculum, so motor car maintenance or cookery might be worth your attention. If you wish to travel abroad, brushing up on a language or starting a new one will be of practical use and enjoyable too. One thing is certain, there is no shortage of new things to have a go at.

Increasing our portfolio of skills and knowledge contributes to our self-worth, especially if others begin to notice the range of interesting things we can do. As with the other behaviours, being proactive is the key, so imbuing your days with a sense of curiosity will help you uncover the learning opportunities which will most suit you. The benefit to your job and future career are obvious.

5. Give

It would appear the adage, 'it is better to give than to receive' has some solid scientific foundation. Here, the advice from the Foresight project is to reach out to others and seek opportunities to offer a helping hand. Polite behaviour is part of this philosophy, smiling at someone, holding a door open, giving up your place in a queue to a person who seems pressed for time, all of these things will be appreciated. The more obvious meaning is significant too. You may decide to donate more to charity, or give money to a homeless person. You will find that both parties benefit from this action.

'Give' is closely linked to 'connect' in this sense, as we try to ensure we are outward looking rather than focusing solely on ourselves. This is a hard thing to do in a society which has something of a 'self' obsession and it may lead us to expect something in return. We may become 'transactional', in our attitude (shopping is now rated as one of the favourite national pastimes). Our natural tendency becomes one where we expect reciprocity.

To counter this there are two things to remember. Firstly, we need to believe 'what goes around comes around', meaning there may not be any direct reward for our giving, but eventually our 'goodness' will come back. Secondly, we are not necessarily just giving to others, in many cases we are giving to ourselves in terms of the increase in our self-esteem.

If we reflect back on an experience like giving up our place in a queue, balance the saving of a few minutes of your time, with being recognised for being kind and, surely, the latter is a much greater reward.

The thread which runs throughout the entire five behaviours programme is one which says, 'take control'. Very often in life we can end up feeling like the victim of someone else's agenda, in work, in a family environment, even socially. It is easy to get out-manoeuvred by others who may wish to force their will upon us. The need to wrest this control back is obvious if we are to influence our own destiny, with particular regard to our happiness and wellbeing.

Erin – public sector team leader

'I know when one of my team is beginning to become 'unwell' in a mental sense. I'm talking here about stress and anxiety. Different people cope with it in different ways, but if someone comes into work looking like they haven't slept, dishevelled, with maybe even their personal hygiene suffering, it's obvious something is wrong in their life.

When we're in control we have our routine, take good care of ourselves, think about the day ahead before it's begun. Having some sway over how we live our lives is critical in keeping us on the straight and narrow'.

Interpreting these behaviours into a coalition of management constructs and adding them into the mix of creating the right environment, getting the right balance between work and home and reaching out to form strong relationships with our staff is the essence of doing the right thing. Although the original work on these behaviours was designed to provide a template for better *personal* wellbeing, it is easy to see their benefit if they are also consciously applied in the workplace.

Conclusions

There are five 'good behaviours' which can enhance our wellbeing

The interrelationship between the behaviours makes them easier to exercise

These things don't happen by chance, you have to make them

Having control is itself a good stress-buster

CHAPTER 14

Environomics

The five behaviours we have looked at form an excellent backdrop to how we might manage ourselves, and our people better. How then do we build on this foundation stone and ensure our workplace is as healthy as it can possibly be?

The first thing to do is get the space right.

The environment and ergonomics of the workplace are really important factors in enhancing or detracting from workers wellbeing. Get them right, and a positive atmosphere is more likely. As you are unlikely to be starting with a blank sheet, where you can design and build a place of work ideally suited to the needs of all the staff, adaptability is the key to success. Being aware of the principles of good practice may help you begin to make alterations, which change things in a positive way.

Sometimes we fail to recognise what is good about our physical workspace. As with many things we begin to take it for granted after a while. Have a quick audit and consider the many positive things about your place of work, rather than seeing it in terms of what you haven't got. Use the notes which follow to guide you through the different aspects of your surroundings.

Don't be downhearted if where you are is not ideal for you or your co-workers, instead celebrate what is good, and be aware of the environmental and ergonomic factors that can improve the way we feel.

Here are some aspects for you to consider.

Personal space

Territory is important in the workplace. However, it is hard to define in the way we may have done a generation ago. Many aspects of the work environment have evolved and changed. Typists used to sit at desks in rows, managers had side offices, sections or departments had a 'footprint' which included their individual work stations, filing cabinets and other paraphernalia.

Some businesses introduced 'booths', each worker sitting at a desk with screens on three sides to block noise and promote privacy. Open plan became the fashion in the 1970s, now we have 'hot desking' and virtual workspace. The physicality of these arrangements is less important than how people feel about them.

A couple of rules apply to the division of space, firstly, is it adequate for the role and secondly, is there parity between employees who perform the same job? Beyond this, the comfort and layout is a matter of common sense, allied to a degree of personal freedom and preference.

Anchors

Part of our personal hierarchy of needs includes a feeling of belonging, and in a real physical sense the workplace can be part of this. A critical factor in people feeling 'emotionally well' about where they work, is the propensity to be 'anchored'. Here are two contrasting stories that illustrate the difference.

Phoebe

'I've worked in local government for 22 years, providing admin support in the main. In spite of lots of bouts of reorganisation, I've had the same desk for the last 7, and that's the way I like it. I can remember our last office move and it was a nightmare, so much stuff just went missing.

I think of my desk as a "home from home", I'm happy in that space and I've got a few little nick-nacks around, to remind me to go home now and again! There are some photos of my loved ones, a couple of postcards that colleagues have sent from their holidays abroad and a clay pot that my grandson made for me.

It's not just about feeling at home though, it's also important to me to have my own operation running smoothly so I don't waste any time looking for things. I've been here so long I have my system sorted'.

Nigel

'We introduced hot desking early last year when we moved to our new premises. I was part of the steering group that debated it, but it was pretty much a done deal, we simply didn't have room for everyone to have their own space.

Lots of us are out on the road for at least some of the time, so there is no longer any logic in having unused desks, it's just increasing the costs of the business without adding value.

At my level, everyone was using a Blackberry and laptop. It's begun to change and a few have switched to iPad, but we know it'll be something new again next year. The point is whatever the device, that's now your workstation, not the physical space you sit in. Even when we're not office based, we're working on trains, at the kitchen table or while waiting in the client's reception area.

If you ask me when I feel "at home", I'd say when I have my laptop on my knee. I could be in the Amazonian jungle for all it matters!'.

Irrespective of our seniority in the organisation, we all share the same need to know where we stand, to have a real sense of where we fit in to the bigger picture and our physical place can contribute greatly to this understanding.

Customisation – somewhere to call 'home'

These examples give us contrasting views about 'anchors'; some people feel all at sea without them, for others, the anchor is more about mind-set than any physical, tangible space.

However, being in a place is only one aspect of feeling at ease, how much ownership we take over it is of equal importance. The references in Phoebe's story to the 'nick-nacks' she has surrounded herself with, are commonplace. In fact one of the difficulties of managing a large office is knowing where to draw the line.

Take a zero tolerance approach, and workers feel oppressed, allow too much leeway and as well as being untidy, the place can become a minefield of health and safety hazards. Consider the purpose of your business, and ask if the level of 'customisation' is appropriate. Banks and solicitors offices tend to have very little; a graphic design company is likely to have an inflatable dinosaur in the corner and a drum kit in the Boardroom!

As well as being part of 'home-making', customisation is important for some as a 'badge of honour'. A personalised workspace can be used to send many signals to co-workers. Photographs, which are one of the most common additions to the personal space can say 'look I have an outside life', or 'I am a contented mother' or 'I have fine, intelligent looking children'.

Ornaments or trophies (of all shapes and sizes), can signal, 'look at me, I'm a bit wacky when I'm not in work', or 'I drive an expensive car' or 'I am a winner'.

Although it may appear that workers have made 'unconscious choices' about what surrounds them, it is often the case that the subconscious mind is attempting to make a significant statement.

Aspect

Having your own bit of territory is important, but it is matched in significance by *which* bit of territory. Desks that are near windows and natural daylight are often feted. Dark cubby holes are to be avoided. So too are areas in proximity to corridors or exits.

Privacy can be vital too, not only for commercial reasons, but personal ones. Sometimes we may need to take a call from a family member, and even if it is not of a particularly sensitive nature, many of us like to keep these things private.

The overall footprint of space is often a source of pride or angst. When staff have been used to having a certain amount of square-footage, they can become very territorial and defensive, if asked to 'budge up a bit' to get an extra desk in.

Often, volume of space can signify status.

Paul

'When I joined the management team we each had our own office. It wasn't long before I discovered an unwritten rule. The number of windows you had signified your place in the hierarchy. I had 2 and was happy with that, I noticed some of my supposed equals had 3 and our boss had 4, which was fair enough.

After a re-shuffle, a new guy took over and to stamp his authority on the post, he had a partition wall removed so that his office had 5 windows!'

Sound, light and the air that we breathe

All the evidence points to detrimental effects of excessive noise in the workplace, for example, above the 85 decibel level, blue collar workers in particular were able to cite more symptoms from a mental health checklist, including anxiety and social dysfunction than colleagues in less noisy environments (McDonald 1989).

Office workers can suffer just as much, not necessarily due to the *volume* of noise, but because of the content. Having to put up with other people's conversations is often given as a reason for reduced output as the distraction it causes makes concentration more difficult (Sundstrom 1986). Workers anecdotally chart their frustration when others 'waste time talking about last night's television', or 'gossip about other people in the office'.

As a manager, balancing these factors can be a minefield. Ban all trivial interactions, and you risk turning the staff into de-motivated automatons, leave things as they are and you may only be operating at half your potential output. Try to take a reasonable and balanced approach.

Noise 'pollution' can be damaging, but so can poor air quality. A range of symptoms can result from air being recycled. So-called 'sick building syndrome' (Cooper et al 2009), can happen as a result of too little fresh air, bringing on symptoms of tiredness, headaches and increased stress, eventually leading to a rise in sickness absence if not addressed.

Connection with nature

It may seem unimportant, but natural daylight and a room with a view are elements of a balanced environment, which workers will really appreciate. Business meetings in the basement of a London hotel are always heavier work than at a country club.

Microsoft in the U.K. have a lake in the grounds of their campus, where staff can go and picnic during the summer months. They even provide a blanket to sit on and free ice-cream, so important do they consider the potential benefit.

Even without the beauty of nature outside, plants and greenery can bring a part of the natural world inside the office and reinvigorate sterile surroundings.

Common land

When we think about the work environment, it is often only in relation to the individual spaces allocated to staff, but this is missing a trick. Some of the most important places in the office are the common areas, the kitchen, around the proverbial 'water cooler' or the staff room. This is where information is exchanged, gossip traded and rumours fuelled, but it is a critical part of the connections which workers make with each other. It can also be a place to let off steam and in that regard is good for de-stressing.

It is sometimes a good idea for management to steer clear and let people claim this space as their own, a kind of safe haven away from the hurly-burly that goes on at their desk. Think of it in terms of a teenager's bedroom, only enter at your own risk!

Detox the desks

The fixed assets of the building may, quite literally, be set in stone, but how the workspace is treated is the responsibility of all who use it. Irrespective of whether it's an office, a factory or a retail space, many hours are simply lost by a lack of organisation.

Sometimes we need to take the time to re-think the pro-cesses we're involved in, to look at them with a critical eye and determine if they are operating at maximum efficiency. Always having to go and search for a piece of often-used equipment, having a printer which is stationed in the wrong part of the office, using till points which are not equipped with all the essentials, all of these things add time, cost and stress.

We acknowledge once more the difficulties of changing the physical environment of the workplace, especially if you are not the one in charge of it. However, there may be some elements which could be put in train, or at least entered into the company suggestion scheme.

A less formal route would be to agree with your immediate boss some remedial action, or call the team together to problem solve, with the common aim of making the environment and ergonomics of work more comfortable and efficient.

Here are some suggestions to kick off your creative thinking:

a. Lead by example – if you're running a team and your personal workspace looks like a bomb has hit it, it shows a lack of organisation and professionalism. It also prevents you from encouraging good discipline in others, or you'll risk coming across with a 'do as I say, not as I do' attitude.

b. Agree some ground rules – call a meeting of your work colleagues and decide between you how you would like to divide up the space, the furniture, plants and tools of your trade. Between you, you will know best how to do this. Be careful not to get into any debates about territory too soon, it will only intimidate people.

c. Sign the pledge – if you have agreed between you that the last five minutes of each day will be 'makeover time', where you put the workspace in good order, ready for the morning, make sure that everyone is signed up to the principle. It only takes one slacker to make the place look a mess!

d. Team clean – starting the process can be daunting, if the accumulated detritus of years of bad practice scatters the landscape. Set a mission of 'bin, archive or keep' for everything around you, then take an hour out one morning where the entire team gets stuck into a collective spring clean and clearout.

e. Encourage parity – try to get staff to see that 'we're all in this together', so petty feuds over the amount of space each of us has are simply a waste of time and effort.

f. Personalise, to a point! – determine between you how much 'desk customisation' should go on, based on what an outsider would think of your business if they dropped in unannounced. A good starting point is to get people to think of it as their home, how would they like others to think they live?

Encouraging the team to come together and display 'house proud' behaviour is part of building the self esteem of individuals within it. Loyalty, a sense of ownership and team working can all be positive outputs from this kind of exercise. More importantly, the state the place is in will not become a distraction from doing the things which matter, either operationally or in the sense of exercising wellbeing behaviour.

Physically de-cluttering can have the knock on effect of clearing the mind, leaving us free to think. This type of practice is commonplace today among organisations which have embraced 'lean' principles of working.

Conclusions

The physical workspace is an important environment for wellbeing

People may feel more grounded if they have a place to call 'home' at work

Customisation is a 'nesting' behaviour

Pride in the way the place looks can lead to pride in the work that's done

CHAPTER 15

Harmonise

The term work-life balance has been a helpful piece of short-hand for a few decades now, but because the nature of work has changed so much, it's becoming redundant. The reason is for many workers, they can no longer segregate either their time or activities into two separate boxes, one with 'work' written on, the other with 'life'.

There are many sociological impacts of this state, with potential damage to health, relationships and productivity all being high risk areas. However the more immediate issue we need to face up to is the effects of long hours on stress.

Although we earlier examined a number of factors in the work-place that lead to more stress, we have not yet considered the effect of being at work for more of the time has.

Contrast the stress levels reported by those who work less than 37 hours a week to a group working in excess of 45 hours. In the latter group exactly twice as many workers reported being stressed, at 46% (only 23% in the low working hours group).

More significant yet is those *claiming* to be very stressed, is three times higher in the long working hours group (17% compared to 5%) (Swan and Cooper 2005).

A further underlying factor that is growing cause for concern is the accuracy with which people report their hours. If, as we have acknowledged, there is more and more cross over between work and home, if emails are being sent and received from trains and buses during the morning and evening commute, if work is carrying on into the evening, how can we accurately chart the working day or week with any degree of confidence.

We come back to technology as the enabler here. Mobility is at the heart of much of it, so portable devices that could once just be used for calls are now broadband enabled, with all the functionality of the computer on our desk, save for a full size keyboard (although this too will be solved in time, probably using better touch screen technology).

But this isn't the whole picture. Those with an office at home used to be confined to a group of mainly senior managers, who had a property big enough to house such a facility and the necessary additional equipment to drive it. Now, as we saw from Nigel's story in the previous chapter, we open up a laptop in the kitchen and our office is right before us. The exponential increase in computer memory over recent years is largely responsible.

Jim – video editor

'Fifteen years ago, we had our digital editing suite fitted out; the technology was brand spanking new at the time. I can remember excitedly stopping colleagues in the corridor to explain that the new system had, wait for it, an entire gigabyte of memory! Back then such capacity was so vast I could hardly comprehend it. I remember thinking we would never need to use it all'.

In the days before we could carry every document we'd ever written or been sent, our working day had a cut off point, once access to our data was left behind in the office. Now, the ease of availability to our documents is at the heart of what we do, when they're only a mouse click or touch screen away, there is always a temptation to dip in.

This can be a good thing, allowing us to use our downtime to keep up. The morning commute can be a long one for city-based workers, so to have the luxury of getting an hour's worth of email out of the way, uninterrupted, before you hit your desk, can be an efficient use of your time.

However, it is the lack of recognition of this time, that was once ours but we have now ceded to our employer, which can lead to problems. Once we get into the habit (and many of us already have) of checking the email inbox at every given opportunity, we may begin to lose track of when we're working and when we're not. The uncomfortable truth may be we're never really switching off, either physically or emotionally. The obvious risk is we may eventually become stressed by all this work. What is less obvious is the dependency we may build up, almost an online addiction. In the nineties, people were reported to need 'post filofax counselling' if they lost their personal organiser, how much worse could this be now, now we carry our lives in a small metal box?

Self importance

A very real danger with technology which allows us to be on 24/7, is we may begin to believe we really are that important. Many reckless individuals already habitually use their cell phones when driving, despite the obvious peril they put themselves and other road users in. Couples in a restaurant may be sharing a romantic meal, until one gets up to use the rest room and the other checks their phone the minute they have departed. Watch the delegates at a conference as they pour out of the hall for a coffee break, like a horde of communication-starved managers, they immediately switch on their mobiles. Perhaps we are all becoming addicted.

Weigh this against the number of time-critical messages we receive, and the behaviour starts to look ludicrous. We're not saying some of this connectedness is not only desirable, or important to our working lives, but more that we are in danger of losing any sense of proportion around it.

If all this is an accurate description of how many of us run our working lives, how can we reclaim some ground, restore some sense of balance, in effect harmonise work with the rest of our activities?

- Diagnosis

A good starting point is to face up to how serious the issue is for you. If you've read the preceding pages nodding to yourself and mentally ticking off the behaviours you exhibit, it may be time to take stock.

For a week, make time to consider what activities you are involved in each day. Chart when the official working day started and ended, make an educated estimate of how much down time you had when you weren't working flat out, and also consider how much extra work you did either before or after the 'official' hours. When you have collected this data, answer the following questions, designed to make you consider if your working life is fair and proportional.

- Workplace expectation

What is in your official contract of employment? How does this tally with the psychological contract, the unwritten expectations that you and your employer have of each other? What is the 'hours culture' of the organisation, does everyone put in the same as you? And finally, make a list of the repercussions of working the hours you do. Are there signs of physical or mental exhaustion, are your out-of-work relationships with family and friends suffering, what might the longer term implications of this be?

Answer these issues without reference to the demands on you, so at this stage do not get hung up on all the reasons *why* you work as hard as you do.

By going through this process you may conclude you want to make some changes in order to try and harmonise your work and 'self time'. It's not necessarily that we begrudge working hard, in fact, it's what makes many of us tick, but there are limits, and it is an empowering feeling to face the reality and decide to make changes.

- Make a plan

Nothing ever got done that wasn't planned for. People study self-help books, research time management techniques on the internet, attend courses on being organised and then expect that by a process of osmosis it will just happen.

For action to take place we have to 'decide it', 'schedule it', 'do it' and 'record it'. With a plan like this, it is useful to make it a two stage process, firstly sit down solo and consider what you would like the future to look like. Secondly, decide how the changes may be made and the benefits that would accrue, then involve the other main parties. This will most likely be your boss, staff and significant external relationships, spouse, partner or family. Having drawn up your plan, put it into train as soon as possible, before you lose momentum. Keep track of progress to maintain your self-motivation.

• Be efficient

One of Stephen Covey's 'seven habits' (Covey 2004), is 'sharpen the saw'. A neat metaphor for working better, not longer and harder. The lumberjacks are sawing a massive tree trunk, sweating and straining for all their worth, unable to take time out to sharpen the saw, but if they did...you can see where it's going.

Now you are at a point when you've decided how much of your time you're prepared to devote to the workplace, it won't necessarily follow that the work load will diminish accordingly, for your convenience. You will need to make tough decisions over what you stop doing, and schedule the rest of your tasks with a more ruthless efficiency.

Setting strict time limits for each task may sound like a strategy to increase stress further, but if you are in control of the process, it's more likely to produce a rush of satisfaction as you knock down your personal targets one by one.

Often, by raising consciousness of the need for efficiency, we begin to see the things that really matter to the running of the business, and all those activities which could best be classed as 'nice to have'. There really isn't room for these any more, and eradicating them from your working day will release time for more mission critical work.

Negotiate

Just because you have made some decisions about the changes you intend to make to your work and your life, it doesn't follow that everyone around you will fall in behind the plan.

However, if you include in your planning process some 'stakeholder analysis', deciding who the key people and how you might best keep them happy, the process is likely to go much more smoothly. Naturally you will need to think of where you might compromise, set targets for best case scenarios, and the least you are prepared to accept. This will help the negotiations go much more smoothly.

This is far from a simple stage. Agreeing some 'core family time' with your spouse and family, where you promise not to be drawn into working, will mean that some similar deal may need to be struck with the boss, so you don't compromise your work position. However, as with many things, people feel much better if they are consulted and involved in a decision making process.

Be firm

Once the 'deals' have been struck, you need to stand by them. Being firm is not only a case of delivering to the important people at work and home, it is also about your self-discipline. Most of us whose work has become de-harmonised, are guilty of contributing to the problem. If we have always responded to emails within an hour, regardless of the time of day, others will think this will continue to be the case. Often, being firm with ourselves is the hardest part.

The process of harmonisation, of taking control so you and those close feel there is a fair balance between the hours you put in at work and the reward, both financial, and in terms of leisure time, is a small part of preparing for better wellbeing.

The real trick is the 'psychological shift', the feeling that you have wrested control back over your life. We all have a bit of the self-destruct about us, never more so than when it comes to time management, but if we are the cause, we are also the cure.

Robin – sales executive

'I had a reputation, among friends and family for always being late. What is a little strange is that I saw it as a great sign of weakness too; I couldn't stand it when others kept me waiting.

Eventually, I came to the conclusion it was all my fault. You can only go on blaming traffic delays for so long before you come to realise you didn't set off in time.

My greatest failing was to believe time would stretch. If I had to depart at ten, I'd think of an unrealistic amount of things I could do between now and then. The last thing on the list would be 'get ready', so instead of showering and dressing first, so that I could walk out of the door at the given hour, I'd leave that until the end. I've not yet beaten my record of 7 minutes to do both, but I was running extremely late that day!

Amazingly I have solved the problem, just by thinking it through'.

There are bound to be times when all this good work on harmonisation goes out of the window. You hit a busy period at work, a pitch needs to be finished, the boss needs answers for her meeting on Monday or a thousand other things. You need to be flexible enough to meet the demands of the business, but by the same token, you will also have to remind yourself at regular intervals of the need to re-harmonise, get the balance back.

As a manager of other people, you have a responsibility to them. If you harmonise your own work and life, it is more likely you will manage better, be less stressed and cope with situations which arise in a calm and measured manner.

By the same token, part of your job is to act as a 'role model for your team'. The impact on them of you running around like a headless chicken, and working all the hours in the day, is they will feel it's a necessary part of their job too. You will be creating a micro-culture which they might feel the need to perpetuate, if they are to avoid letting you down.

So, by changing the way you work, it's highly likely they will do the same, hopefully for the better wellbeing and greater efficiency of the department as a whole.

What underpins the necessity for harmonisation is the need to make time to consciously exercise wellbeing behaviours (connect, take notice, be active, learn, give), rather than being swept up in an agenda set by other people, which is out of your control.

Often we feel swept along in the workplace, unable to alter the status quo. By attempting small, but regular changes, with determination and by re-affirming the benefits on a regular basis, much more self-empowerment can take place than we may have believed.

Conclusions

You owe some of yourself to work and some to leisure, you should be the one who decides

Plan a new way of working and stick to it

Involve other stakeholders in the process; they're more likely to support you

Use the time you save to exercise wellbeing behaviours

CHAPTER 16

Training your brain

Two critical elements of set-up are in place. Establishing the right working environment was the first, then finding time for ourselves by harmonising work and home, taking control over our lives once more, is the second building block.

Now having put the groundwork in place, what are we going to do, both for ourselves and our staff, in order to drive home some of the essential wellbeing behaviours which have been identified?

Let us begin with a look at our overall mental and physical health, and consider how we might stimulate both.

Curiosity

Lifelong learning has become something of a mantra in the work-place over recent decades and apart from it being a 'worthy' objective, its seeming effects on greater wellbeing are becoming more apparent as scientific investigation and research gather pace and weight.

There is certainly evidence to suggest that in later years the adage 'use it or lose it' is much more than folklore. Those with higher levels of stimulating brain activity, seem better able to slow the effects of degenerative mental conditions such as Alzheimer's disease. Maybe we'd all be better for a game of chess a day!

By the same measure it appears what is good for the aged is good as well throughout our lives, and conveniently, it fits well with the expectations of the workplace. Most employers are looking for staff who are ambitious enough to want to progress. The current view is we should 'recruit for attitude, train for skill' (no surprise in an economy dependent on service led jobs), so some degree of 'learned skill' is clearly necessary once the selection process has been completed.

There need be no limit to this, and if this case arises, the well-being benefits can be sustained over time. There are many reasons why learning new knowledge contributes to our mental capital. Part of the picture is the process itself, but there is more. Our self-esteem may be boosted by having acquired greater insight, and this can also have a 'knock-on effect' with social skills, as we have a broader range of topics we are able to discuss. Promotion in work might ensue, increasing our standard of living, giving us higher status among our peers and developing a greater sense of self worth.

Are we better people for knowing more? It would appear so. What then are the essential aspects of learning?

Interest

Inherent in the term 'curiosity', is a sense of interest in what is going on round about us. This continual stimulation is part of the feeling of being 'alive'. The more we use it, the greater our awareness of the world.

Without the input of such stimulus, we can find ourselves stagnating.

Elspeth – administrative support

'I suppose I should have moved on a year or two before I did, it was laziness really which prevented me. I'd been working in the same office for 12 years, which seems amazing when I think back; it just sort of crept up on me.

> Then one day, I was so unbelievably bored and I realised that I'd become stuck in a rut. It's strange when I look back at photos of me then, I'd put on lots of weight, my clothes were a mess, so was my hair, it was like I'd lost interest in everything, not just the work. I actually think I looked unsuccessful; I wore it like a kind of badge.
>
> I've vowed never to do that again. Right now work and for that matter life is much more interesting and I'm even happy with the way I look…well sort of!'

We have already touched on the importance of forming connections, and it is worth recognising here that our ability to link up the relationships in our lives, and to form new alliances, is very much dependent on our willingness to be interested in others. Even before we get to that stage, it helps if we are interested in ourselves.

Knowledge

We have seen how the acquisition of knowledge can be of benefit to us, and our organisation. In a practical sense it makes us better able to do our jobs, which has a major impact on our status.

But maybe knowledge goes beyond this, and is simply good for us, for its own sake. As we get older we feel the benefit of life experience in helping us to make sense of our world.

Youth may have the advantages of energy and beauty, but maturity and knowledge bring a sense of greater calm, an ability to take decisions with more confidence and the resilience borne out of knowing you've been here before.

Organisations have only woken up to the phenomenon of 'knowledge management' in recent times, realising that the accumulated wisdom of many older workers is a valuable asset and something that should be nurtured and farmed.

'Knowledge is power'.

Variety

No matter how enriching any individual experience, the repetition of it is bound to dim the enjoyment. In the movie *Groundhog Day*, Bill Murray plays a journalist who wakes up to the same day over and over. The humour in the film is based around his attempts to relieve the boredom by changing his own response to the 'sameness' which is going on around him.

A different route to work, a change in our usual diet, or an activity we wouldn't normally consider can all break the cycle of routine for the better. Part of the ageing process is often a tendency to stick to regular patterns, and those who are 'old before their time' tend to be typified by being set in their ways.

'Variety is the spice of life'.

Infinity

If curiosity is made up of the elements we've identified, interest, knowledge and variety, then the virtuous circle can be created by 'infinity', which is to suggest that if we are truly curious, there are no boundaries.

Our natural inquisitiveness, if exploited to its' most heightened will never be constrained by limits, there will always be something more to discover. Man's ability to problem solve, to find answers to medical conditions, to invent and to develop is underpinned by this principle.

'Let's boldly go where no man has gone before!'

With these ideas in place, it is hard not to get excited about learning. However, the content is still likely to be the single biggest factor in turning us on to new knowledge.

What to learn?

The most fantastically energising aspect of adult learning is choice. Our schooldays were different when we had a set curriculum, the workplace mimics this to an extent as we are required to learn the different aspects of our jobs. Even here, with the many and varied ways of taking knowledge on board, there is a degree of freedom. Aside from this rather narrow part of our learning, the world is ours to embrace in whatever way we wish.

There is no template for what to learn, it is up to you, but we have detailed some categories you may wish to consider, while at the same time thinking about how, when and where your learning might take place.

This section contains thought-provoking ideas about the following learning types

- Agility
- Practitioner knowledge
- Personal development
- Creative learning
- Nice-to-learn

Agility

Think of your brain as a trapeze artiste, leaping from swing to swing, stretching every sinew in order to achieve your goal. It is the kind of activity which is good for slowing down the onset of age related cognitive disorders, which we outlined earlier.

Games consoles manufacturers have long understood this idea, developing a range of activities that are mentally stretching, but fun at the same time, with the idea you have a short burst of activity each day, to train your brain to be better.

More traditional methods of taxing our grey matter have been around for much longer, a crossword puzzle will stimulate thought, logic and problem solving, all the more so if cryptic. Newspapers now often have a 'games' section, which will also include number games, word puzzles, or posers in the form of a dummy chess game or a hand of bridge.

It is hardly surprising that the internet also provides a rich source of similar material; there's something for everyone. Try searching under 'brain teasers' and 'brain training', between them they yield over ten million results, enough for most of us.

The greatest benefit from this type of learning derives from doing it daily. Not only does this allow for our skill to build, one 'brain-trained brick at a time', but it provides a tiny oasis of 'me-time', important in the battle against stress.

You can either set a time of day when you will always go through your mental agility workout, or use it as a 'reward', incentivising you to finish the particular piece of work you're doing before taking ten minutes out.

If used as a regular pattern of routine, your daily 'exercise' can be a contributor to stress reduction. If you always have a crack at the crossword when you first get home, it can provide a 'bridge' between the working day and a more relaxed evening, helping you to wind down.

You may also find over time, your ability to analyse complex information and come to decisions improves, helping you at work as well as at home.

Practitioner knowledge

This is the kind of learning which fits into the category of continuous professional development (CPD), of the sort championed by many organisations. As well as providing a platform for increasing knowledge that is directly mapped to the competencies required for our role, it can be a fantastic motivational tool as well.

When an employer invests time and/or money in a member of staff, it is an indication of their faith in them and a desire to increase their skills, and consequently, their worth in the organisation. Often it is a forerunner to promotion and though this may not occur directly following a training intervention, it can be said, over time, to contribute to the value the organisation places on the individual.

A natural tendency is to think of this kind of learning in terms of the conventional training course, perhaps because this is the way training and development managers have traditionally achieved their aims. There is increasing recognition that other forms of learning can be just as powerful, or even more so.

A range of 'blended' learning solutions are available, which may include some time in the classroom, but also demand some self-study, either from text books, or more likely these days, online.

On the job training is also powerful, 'learning the ropes' from someone who has been doing the job for a while. If the formal training budget in your organisation is restricted, think in terms of other methods of knowledge transfer, like work shadowing, mentoring or even reading up around your job role from the internet or library. It's an investment in your future, and often energising in its own right.

Personal development

We may rightly expect our employer to invest in us, for their good and ours, but we can also take the initiative when it comes to learning. Aside from professional skills, which might be underpinned by a desire to get on, we all have gaps in our knowledge which we can benefit from filling.

People often return to the topics they never quite mastered at school. This might be because, later in life, we come to realise the elements of say mathematics, or a language which might be essential to our development. It may also to be down to stubbornness, where we 'refuse to be beaten'!

Learning doesn't have to be constrained by subjects in the F.E. college syllabus. We may instead be curious about the ever changing world around us. If so there is no shortage of media outlets, which can help you become a 'news junkie'.

Throughout life, we grow as people by a combination of what we learn and the things we experience. Making a conscious effort towards this state is a key feature of increased wellbeing.

Creative learning

Allied to our proactive approach to taking on board more intellectual knowledge, is the chance we have every day to begin learning a new creative skill. The spread of topics is as diverse as the world we live in. How about learning to play a musical instrument? What about water colour painting, sugar craft, pottery, circus skills (juggling is easier than you think, uni-cycling harder!), singing, conjuring, hairdressing, the list goes on.

Many of these things can be classed as hobbies, but they are no less useful or rewarding because of that. Indeed, they can complement our more cerebral pastimes, at work or home, to deliver a balance of activities. This can be an excellent way of relieving stress, taking ourselves off into another world where we cease to think about the daily problems we might encounter in the workplace. As an aside, they're sometimes quite good for showing off your willingness to take on unusual challenges!

Nice-to-know

This final category is a catch all for learning which does not fit elsewhere. We recognise the fact we live in an age of information overload, and if nothing were ever printed again, novel, magazine, textbook or newspaper, we still wouldn't have enough life left to get through all we wanted.

The question is, have we any room for being non-selective. Surrounded with so much rich media and knowledge which is relevant to our lives, do we really have time to consume anything frivolous?

If we are not to stagnate into dull automatons, the answer is yes. Pap, tittle-tattle and trivia are mindless antidotes to our serious side. Celebrity culture may well have got out of hand, but there isn't any harm in knowing which A-lister has married which up-and-coming, or who is getting the attention of the general public. This comes with a warning; it should be consumed in measured amounts, as part of a balanced diet!

And this is a good place to end a section on learning. Important messages emerge. Useful learning will only happen as a consequence of identifying our personal gaps, and planning to fill them. A blend of different types of learning is good in developing us as people. There will always be more to learn, so endeavour to be selective in what you choose, and remember to sometimes give yourself some time off to pick up the facts which contribute to you being a 'mine of useless information', it's all about balance.

Here's a final word about learning, sometimes in order to find out new things we will need to be nosey (some would say curious!). There is nothing wrong with this in a workplace environment, because as a manager, it will mean you have to do more listening. Whatever the difficulties our staff may face, however tough the economic conditions we are operating in, they want their voices heard. When we take the time to listen, we learn.

Conclusions

Lifelong learning is part of the mantra of many organisations; it's good to show willing

If knowledge is not exactly power, it is certainly powerful

Choose a variety of new things to learn, some for work and some for you

Frequent 'stretching' of our brain power is thought to slow down degenerative mental conditions

CHAPTER 17

Activity and fitness

With your mind in the best shape it can be, what about your body? Exercise is good for you, this much is inarguable. The link between increased fitness and a reduction in likelihood of a number of physiological conditions, such as heart disease, diabetes and obesity is now accepted (Lundberg and Cooper 2010). For some time, there has been a feeling that there are positive benefits in a psychological sense too, but there is less research available to back this up to date.

That said, the generality of the arguments are accepted, it is the specifics of which kind of exercise is best for treating individual ailments which remains under scrutiny.

In the early nineties the International Society of Sport Psychology agreed with America's National Institute of Mental Health on the general issue. They stated that they believed specific conditions, like anxiety, stress and depression, could be alleviated by way of regular exercise. Those suffering from depression tended to have a more sedentary lifestyle, and in studies of patients with this condition they have reported the exercise part of their treatment programmes to be the most significant element in alleviating the symptoms.

Even a non-scientific view points us towards some common sense benefits, outside any possible changes in brain function. Exercise is something which is largely conducted outside the workplace, and allows little room for multi-tasking, although you occasionally see people on the gym treadmill, cell phone in hand!

As an important element of self-esteem, working hard to get our bodies in shape is almost like a reward in itself. Any physical changes we may see over time, loss of weight, building of muscle, toning of our bodies etc. will add to this, as these are generally recognised as signs of attractiveness.

Although some exercise can be undertaken on a solo basis, like road running or an aerobics regime done at home, it is for many people a social practice. Competitive activity brings us into contact with opponents and partners, in things like racquet sports. Even a gym workout can be done with friends, who might share in the social benefits once the exercise regime is over.

It is therefore little wonder that 'be active' appears on the list of five behaviours designed for better wellbeing. How though do we incorporate this into our working lives? We can't set up a tennis court in the office, so are there strategies we can adopt to help us in our pursuit of physical exercise?

Shift your mind first – getting fit and keeping fit takes time. This is one of the principle reasons why many regimes fail, other things, work and life principally, get in the way. Part of the reason for this is we see exercise as a kind of add on, a nice-to-have, but only if we've got the time. Really successful programmes rely on our ability to see exercise as an essential part of our routine, not for it's own sake, but because of what it gives us.

If we don't do this, there is a risk of an hour at the gym seeming like a luxury we haven't the time to afford. However, if we take that same hour and think of it as part of keeping us at our peak, not just physically, the investment in time is much easier to justify.

If the exercise time helps us stay balanced and unstressed, then the benefit might be a more productive day at work, better relationships with your spouse and children, a more harmonious way of life altogether. Now the time out for exercise doesn't seem so indulgent.

So, get your mindset right and you will increase the chances of getting your body fit.

Building routine without boredom – there is general agreement over the best kind of exercise regimes. They happen a little and often, it's no good doing nothing all week and bingeing at the weekend! Current advice includes a target of 30 minutes exercise for 5 days of every week.

If you think you can only manage a couple of structured sessions, like a visit to the gym or a game of badminton, you need to consider the way the rest of your time is spent, in order to build exercise into what you do. Any activity which leaves you slightly breathless and heated counts, so household chores or gardening could both be part of your regime. If, in order to raise your heart rate, you throw yourself into mowing the lawn or vacuuming the carpet, the added bonus is it will be done quicker, so you'll contribute to better health and more efficient time management in one go.

You can make exercise part of your daily commute; walk or cycle all or part of the journey. If you take a bus or train, get off a stop early and when you are at work, stop taking the lift, use the stairs instead.

With a bit of inventive thinking, you will soon come up with different ways you can stay active, without taking lots of time out of your day, challenge yourself to integrate exercise into what you'd normally do.

For the first month of this new regime, keep a record of how and when you have amassed your exercise time. This will help consolidate the activity and give you the impetus to keep up the good work.

Introduce competition (gently) – Many find the best way of exercising is through sport and, if that is your preference, you may be able to rope your work colleagues in by starting a league for a racquet sport like tennis or squash. Alternatively a quick internet search will yield results of what is available for team sports, like football or hockey in your area, so you could link up with workmates and enter into the activity that way.

An innovative way of encouraging others to join you is by taking on a team initiative such as the Corporate Global Challenge (www.gettheworldmoving.com), an initiative which began in Australia to improve organisations' wellbeing. Essentially it is a team based challenge to 'walk the world' by taking 14,000 steps per day over 16 weeks, measured via pedometer. The challenge allows participants to track their progress via the website and offers motivational tips along the way. If this seems like a step too far (no pun intended), do some research into charities of your choice and see if you can raise money through some other kind of physical challenge. Lots organise sponsored bike rides or runs.

Having a competitive and/or team element is great for keeping us going. Just make sure it doesn't get too competitive, or you will undo all the good wellbeing work!

Integrate your activity – Using some of the techniques we have talked about, try to ensure even this competitive element is a part of your working life, not a 'bolt on', otherwise it will soon become a chore and fall off the agenda.

By introducing a team ethos, you have an opportunity to build relationships in work, effectively connecting better with other people (another wellbeing discipline which we have talked about). This is even better if you can include other departments as the social contact may help to break down the traditional functional 'silos', which people often operate in.

If you can gather some momentum behind your actions, you could think about approaching your occupational health department, and see if a grander initiative could be planned. Perhaps some kind of sports-credits could count towards time off. Alternatively you could hold a summer sports day, mixing more serious challenges with some fun activities. Some companies do this, and introduce an additional element of competition by inviting suppliers to submit teams too.

Another part of integrating your sport is to consider when in the day you will participate. Some early birds manage a swim or gym session before they go to work, most of us are too busy. Consider if you could get a game of squash in at lunchtime (see below for 'reclaiming your lunch hour'). If your workplace has no shower facilities, you may need to gather a few colleagues together and begin to lobby the management team, they are more likely to invest if they see a genuine fitness initiative from a few of you.

With creativity and the will to look after ourselves, we can soon overcome the sedentary lifestyle which has become part and parcel of many of our working lives, and the benefits to the individual and the organisation means these schemes pay for themselves.

Take a lunch hour – An increasing number of office workers have given up lunch hour, thinking it will help them get through their workload, many now grab a snack and eat at their desk.

Apart from being bad for you, it turns out in lots of cases it is also bad for business. Lunchtime is seen by many as a point in the day when you take on some food to keep your energy levels up; it can be so much more.

As Leonardo da Vinci suggested, 'to remain constantly at work will diminish your judgement. Go some distance away, because work will be in perspective and a lack of harmony is more readily seen'.

At a fundamental level you will need some time to eat, if you can do this away from your desk, or preferably away from the office altogether, you will have a much better chance of enjoying and properly digesting your food. It may be that you take a packed lunch or normally grab a sandwich, but eating it while sitting on a park bench is much better than in front of your computer.

It is also true that taking time out to eat properly is much more likely to cut down on the unhealthy 'grazing', which office-based workers are often prone to, you could lose weight!

The psychological break from the office is also a chance to reflect on the morning's activities and map out the afternoon's, with the potential bonus of reducing your stress through better planning. During your 'reflective time', you have an additional opportunity to put some real perspective on what you have been doing and this can help to reduce the weight of many problems.

Finally, if you get out at lunchtime you may have the chance to exercise, even a stroll will be better than being sat at your desk.

This advice is easier to follow in summer time when the weather is good; there may be much less incentive to go out in the wind and rain. However, if you begin to re-claim the ground of lunchtime (it's your time, written down in your contract of employment), you can legitimately use it for your activities. Now you have an hour a day to catch up on some reading, do your online banking, or plan a holiday. All these activities will provide a proper break between periods of work and if done right will help to increase your productivity in the afternoon, so everyone gains. A couple of days a week, you could even arrange to have lunch with colleagues, getting to know them as individuals, rather than roles.

Looking after ourselves is not just about exercise, although it plays a major part. We also need to take care of ourselves in other ways too. A healthy diet and the avoidance of too much alcohol, will also help. If you are a smoker, it could be time to think about quitting. Try to get ample sleep, drink enough water to avoid de-hydrating (the current advice is to drink when we're thirsty, not force litres into our system).

All of this is sensible and well known. The important thing is to consider it in line with the rest of your life and your personality. We have all seen people who have dieted too much, others whose abstinence has made them miserable. So don't let your desire for wellbeing fight with your propensity to be happy, as has often been said before 'moderation in all things'.

Conclusions

Exercise is good for us

We are more likely to stick to a regime if we plan it, or if there is a competitive element

Involve as many other people at work as possible, they and the organisation will benefit

You may end up being better connected as a result of this activity

CHAPTER 18

Embrace

We have now examined the physical environment of the office, thought through the implications of harmonising our work and leisure selves and considered ways of keeping our minds and bodies in good shape.

These thoughts and deeds form the backdrop for changing the way we work. Without them, it's likely that any new behaviours we attempt to adopt will at best be short term.

The final piece of our jigsaw is to look at how we make and sustain strong connections with people around us. We have called this behaviour 'embrace', as it seeks to build in the positive elements of inclusiveness through better connections and an openness to giving more of ourselves, not necessarily in terms of time, but in attitude.

Connectivity, such a hot topic in the world of technology, has paradoxically dropped down our human agenda in work, as many of us became too busy to really give it any attention. Everyone has heard tales of colleagues who work a few desks from each other sending email, rather than connecting face-to-face. Making the effort to stay personally connected takes time, and few of us have much of that precious commodity any more. The problem is exacerbated by a waning *ability* to make connections, there is a 'use it or lose it' rule which applies, and for many time-starved workers, they have failed to use it enough in the past. So, we are faced with re-learning what making connections is about. At the very heart of this ethos is an action which has fallen into short supply, it is that of 'giving'.

It isn't that we are mean-spirited, we have simply become conditioned by society and culture to look for reciprocity in our giving, rather than offering simply because it's the right thing to do. Our lives are made up of bargaining, we strike a deal with our employer called a contract of employment, we shop around for goods, if not actually haggling in store, we trade one supplier off against another when we are online, similarly we bargain with our children and our partners in order to reach compromise. With all this going on, it is not surprising that when we give, we expect to receive.

However, once we 'pledge to give' in a way that requires no direct return from the other party, we have set ourselves up to have the power to make a difference, we cease to be dependent on assessing the 'return on investment', and free ourselves of it's burden.

Become an activist

If you really believe in making things better, you will need to begin by re-framing who you are, a change of thinking is needed. The terms 'activist' and 'pacifist' are usually applied to war and conflict situations. If we think of our campaign to do the right thing as a 'battle', then it's appropriate terminology.

Nothing ever got done by people sitting on the sidelines, so the future is going to have to start with you. In this context, pacifism is akin to apathy. It is almost by default that the people who end up at the periphery are the culture victims, having to fit in because of their lack of willingness to do anything about the current status quo. These are the people we are going to begin influencing in a positive way.

In this group, there will be a small percentage of what we might call 'the great disengaged'. There are people in all organisations who have ceased to function in any meaningful way, and only manage to get through the tedium of each day by criticising everything that passes through their field of vision. Better, faster progress will be made if you devote your efforts to those people who can be influenced and motivated. Try to stop worrying over the lost causes, they will only sap your energy and batter your resilience.

If, for the sake of argument, you manage a team of eight people, you could start by ranking them in terms of the positivity of their attitude. Having done this, it makes sense to convert your number 1 person first, as it takes the least effort, when it comes to working on the second name on the list, you already have the support of another and this momentum grows the further down the rankings you go. If you begin at the other end, believing 'if I can convert the worst one, I can convert any of them', you will be much more likely to run out of steam before you get past first base.

Using activism, we have an opportunity to create a culture that is at the heart of the word 'embrace'. There are a number of actions you can take which will help to get you started.

Model the right behaviour

There is inherent satisfaction in doing the right thing and if at the most basic level this makes us more of a 'good citizen' either in work or out, the level of inclusion we attract is likely to rise. Which of us wouldn't choose to spend time with someone who is kind and thoughtful, over another who is complacent and lazy?

Using the backdrop of this word 'embrace', we can start to look for everyday situations where we can offer a helping hand, a word of encouragement or the proverbial 'arm round the shoulder' to someone else.

In one study after another, when workers cite the characteristics of great management, words and phrases like 'integrity' and 'living the values' crop up. The same in parenthood, when we model the behaviour we believe is right, it is easy for it to be copied.

Listen

As managers we are forever being told to listen, but how often do we do it in a way that really matters. Thinking about the feelings, motivations and lives of other people should give us an insight to who they are, and if we really actively listen to what they tell us, we will start to understand what is important to them.

If a member of the team asks to leave early to attend their child's school sports day, use this as an 'embrace' opportunity. When they return to work the next morning take what amounts to only a few seconds out of your schedule to ask about the event, 'did they enjoy it?', 'were the children exhausted afterwards?' 'what was the funniest part of the event?'

This kind of behaviour is really memorable for people, and by taking the time to listen, you increase the likelihood of them listening to you in return.

Some managers learn by rote the names of the families of their staff, as if it's some kind of trick. It's much better if you can be genuine about your 'embracing' behaviour.

Act (not intend)

How often have we 'meant to send so-and-so a get well card', or text a timely 'good luck' message to a friend? The reality is, intention is worthless, 'it's action which matters'.

Where possible exercise a 'do it now' policy, so act the minute you think of it. Failing this you need some kind of reminder to alert you, and most cell phones have this facility within the diary or alarms/alerts menu. If your pal's interview isn't until next Thursday, set up the reminder for Wednesday afternoon and send that text the minute it beeps.

Similarly in work situations, intending to thank someone isn't the same as doing it, and often it is words, backed by the thoughtfulness to deliver them, which are seen as greater motivators than money or gifts.

Tune in

Some people are naturally empathetic and insightful, they can read characters and tell when someone is going through a bad time, it's something of a gift. For the rest of us, we have to make a conscious effort to 'tune in', but like so many things, the more practice we get, the easier it becomes.

A little like active listening, this action is one which requires some concentration, but instead of observing just what's 'on the lines', we need to think about what is also 'between the lines'. Often body language, demeanour and mood signal how someone is feeling inside, despite the brave face they may be showing to the world.

Keep your antenna fully operational and they will 'learn' to spot the mood swings at work. You will then know when more 'embrace' behaviour is needed.

Keep

We have the capacity to remember many things, but often we choose the wrong ones. The positive experiences we are part of, or even better, instigate, are worth our attention, and we should try to store them away.

We can avoid the pitfall of this becoming a 'smug-bank', where we have filed all our good deeds, or compliments we have received, instead look on it as a store of positivity, something to call upon when we ourselves are under pressure and in need of a boost to our resilience. Being able to visit our past positive experiences, is a way of keeping us connected to others and maintaining our self esteem.

Reflect

Make a little time for yourself now and then, to recall some of these positive experiences you have salted away. Just the memory of something happy can trigger happiness in the moment. We know this to be the case, if we reminisce with family or enjoy a school reunion.

It's equally possible to achieve on your own, but it won't happen by chance, it needs a slot in your schedule. Think of it as 'wellbeing time'.

Activism takes energy, and when we're not succeeding in changing things we can lose heart and give up. It is only by reminding ourselves along the journey of the good things we've achieved and of the higher purpose of our actions, that we can maintain resilience against the odds.

The ethos of 'embrace' takes in some of the recommended behaviours from the Foresight project's five behaviours, like 'connect' and 'give', but adds an encompassing element to it. In order to effectively implement some of these principles, you will have to squeeze them tight to get the most out of them.

Perhaps the most important action of all is to 'keep listening' all the time, so you can get regular updates on how things are progressing. It is all well and good giving your staff the opportunity to connect, but it has to be with the right things, otherwise they will become apathetic or feel patronised. Without the right connections your actions will simply be seen as 'moving the deckchairs on the Titanic'.

By continually asking the question about the effectiveness of your actions, you will be making more connections of your own, and be influencing your personal wellbeing as a result.

Conclusions

The spirit of 'embrace' is about giving of ourselves to connect better

A little personal activism goes a long way

Keep your eyes and ears open and tune into opportunities to embrace

The effort you expend is 'wellbeing time'

CHAPTER 19

Re-affirmation

When changes are proposed in the workplace, there is one unwavering element which is never far away. The questions that greet new ideas are, 'what will it cost?' and 'how much will it save?'

Wouldn't it be much more productive if someone took the time to ask, 'what will it do?' This broader enquiry seeks to discover the far reaching consequences of the actions, in terms of a wide set of variables. This might include the effect on morale (Bowles and Cooper 2009), or stress levels, how self-esteem might be damaged or improved, what the outside perceptions of the company are, what attitudinal shifts might occur in customers or suppliers. Eventually we get down to the cost implications, they are of course important, but so are the other considerations.

Creating an alliance of 'the right thing' does not require much in terms of direct costs, it is mostly about a shift in attitudes. This has become increasingly important in modern business, because as we acknowledge, the nature of work has shifted from manufacturing to service. In this new economy, craft skill is less important than behaviour, and if this can be moved in a positive direction, the business should benefit.

Lynda – First line manager

'Telephone banking is less prevalent than it once was, due to a switch towards online account management, but at it's height I ran a team of operators. As well as the technical skill to handle transactions, much of what we tried to instil was to do with customer engagement.

Training courses can take you so far, but in the end, it is the personality and judgement of the individual which is critical, I did my best to empower my team and trust them to do the right thing.

I had one woman who noticed a large sum had been paid into a customer's account and when she had finished handling his routine transactions, asked if he would marry her. She was joking of course, but the level of rapport with that customer couldn't be replicated by anyone else. That's what I call discretionary behaviour'.

The will of employees to do this can be increased by constantly encouraging 'the right thing', This will bring real meaning to recommendations like 'connect' and 'give', allowing individuals their own freedom to interpret the behaviour as they think fit, for the benefit of themselves, their colleagues, and the customers.

In a retail environment this might be as simple as carrying an elderly shopper's goods to their car, or in a call centre, it might require the employee to go 'off script' either to better engage with a customer or offer additional helpful advice.

In service industries where customer engagement and long term relationships are of paramount importance, the exercising of discretionary behaviour in this way is a route to optimising performance.

But it's not in the script, so in order to encourage employees to behave in this way, we need to win their hearts as well as their minds. To instigate and drive these changes home, let us recap and consider some of the compelling reasons behind them. This will help us to re-affirm our intent and provide a rationale to any doubters we may meet along the way.

Work is life

It is only the most mundane of roles which now allows the post holder the luxury, (if it can be called that), of delineating between work and leisure. Repetitive manual tasks do still exist, but in lower numbers now 'machines' have been programmed to take their place in many instances (think of motor industry production lines).

In these roles, the low demand on mental capacity, and lack of emotional engagement, gives workers the opportunity to be in the place of work for eight hours a day, without investing anything of themselves in what they do. Real life returns the moment they walk out of the door, but levels of fulfilment are very low and the individuals concerned can be deemed to be simply 'marking time' while they wait for their next pay cheque.

But for many more workers, the dividing line has all but disappeared, and the expectation many of us put on ourselves, is that we have forsaken our right to uninterrupted leisure. Some see this manifested in purely physical ways, like the constant checking of the Blackberry, or report writing at home, but there is an even more pervasive, hidden form of work going on. This takes the guise of thinking about, worrying over and ruminating on what has happened today, how that will affect tomorrow and the longer term future. After a long hard day at the office, many will (eventually), remove themselves physically from the environment, but take part of the trials and tribulations home inside their head.

The lack of clear blue water between the workplace and home life has resulted in the inarguable fact that for many people 'work is life'.

Breadwinner and home maker

The ongoing revolution which has done much to bring equality for men and women has spurned the spin-off of 'role confusion'. Distant fathers whose sole role is breadwinner and stay-at-home mum's, are much harder to find these days for sociological and economic reasons.

If all Dad had to do was 'bring home the bacon', his contribution to the household was limited to financial support only. Now it's recognised that a crucial part of fulfilled family life, is the involvement of fathers across a broad spectrum of activities. Equally, mothers whose role was home-making, now have greater demands than ever as they try to balance elements of child rearing and work. No matter how far we think we've moved, all the evidence still suggests women bear the brunt of housework and looking after children, as well as now having to contribute financially (Lewis and Cooper 2005).

We have seen there is increasing evidence that a person who returns from work in a stressed state, passes this straight to their partner at home, even if they have had a 'happy' stress free day. The necessity for both parties to the relationship to have 'wellbeing' days at work is greater than ever.

Civic duty

Even when we are part of the corporate machine, carrying out duties according to the contract of employment, we have contact, influence and responsibility with regard to our co-workers or our staff.

It is true that stress levels can be adversely affected by workload, but it is much more usual that there is some human factor at play, a negative emotional intervention which underpins the angst.

We probably don't think about this weighty responsibility to our co-workers often enough or deeply enough, yet in most enterprises, it is the relationship staff have with their colleagues which goes a long way to determining how happy they are at work, or conversely, how stressed. Relationships matter to both sides, and they don't get left behind when people come home at night. We can, therefore, conclude that how we treat people at work will influence their wellbeing, both during the day and in their private life.

Self actualisation

Abraham Maslow (1954), used this term to describe the highest point in his hierarchy of needs. A sense of oneness, it can be driven to a large degree by the satisfaction we derive from being successful at work. As we no longer have to hunt for food, establishing status is a much more significant need, in our modern world and it is interlinked with our day jobs. We may be admired and loved at home for being a great spouse or a fantastic parent, but beyond this unquestioning family adoration, where else but work do we acquire such positive affirmation?

As well as providing the money we need to survive, work has become inextricably linked with our self-worth, increasingly it governs who we are, not only in terms of how others view us, but how we also see ourselves. With this level of importance placed on our roles, it is clear to see how wellbeing at work is an intrinsic part of how fit, healthy and happy we are overall.

The very fact work itself can make us happy, necessitates a counter-balancing health warning. If our emotional wellbeing is partly dependent on the status we gain at work, what would happen if that were taken away?

David (42) – Sales Director

'I didn't see it coming, which is ironic really as I'd been the one who had made staff redundant left, right and centre. I actually thought I was too important to be got rid of. Even aside from doing the dirty work of handling redundancies, I really did believe that my contribution was so significant they'd never risk losing me.

Part of that belief system was based on the effort I put in, always first to the office in the morning, I never left until 8 p.m. So I guess I just convinced myself that it'd never happen to me.

When the axe fell, the effects were so devastating that in the end I had a breakdown, I just couldn't cope with going from hero to zero overnight'.

Work can be a powerful influence in our lives and the more time we spend there, the greater the potential to alter the entire mood of our existence. Organisations have a 'duty of care' to the employees, they must take reasonable steps to ensure their safety and keep them from harm. We have to take our part in this too, ensuring where possible we look after ourselves, exercise a duty of care in relation to our own wellbeing, but also be aware of how our behaviour may affect the lives of others in our charge.

Conclusions

It is sometimes better to think of what change will do, rather than how much it will cost

Work and life are inextricably linked, we have a duty to make them both harmonious

Changing gender roles have put more pressure on both sexes with regard to work

Much of our self-worth is developed and nurtured in the workplace

CHAPTER 20

Action

There is a lot to take in, but don't despair, this isn't boot camp for happiness. You do not have to make wholesale changes to your attitudes or behaviour, either in work or out, not overnight. All the evidence shows us that small changes, sustained over time become part of our routine and once embedded, they stick.

It will also be the case that you are already acting in the way the research suggests across some of the defined behaviours, perhaps you take exercise every day, or you may be the kind of person who goes out of their way to make connections. It is not as if everything is broken.

However, we have also recognised the trend towards increased work-based stress. We have the ability and knowledge to improve wellbeing, but we also have the responsibility. Things won't get better for us in the workplace unless we make them.

Seize the day – (self empowerment)

Begin by recognising that there's a difference between empowerment and authority. There might be a set limit to the latter, governed by our job role. With the former, empowerment, it is also true that hierarchy can play its' part, inasmuch as the boss can bestow additional authority upon us. However, we can also empower ourselves by the simple process of deciding to do so.

This is especially important in relation to organisational culture, and the powerful effect it has on governing our behaviour. One of the key elements of this is the recognition that there are many things which happen in the workplace, where no written rule pertains; in a sense there is nothing to say you *shouldn't* do things differently.

Apply a light touch to changes, and you will be surprised at how many of them go unnoticed. If you follow the advice in the chapter about shifting culture, you should begin to notice some discernable differences within your field of influence in a matter of months.

Act responsibly, and it is highly likely no one will question your behaviour. Remember there isn't a rule to cover every eventuality, sometimes it is up to you to make your own.

Grace

'I've worked a lot with public sector bodies, sometimes in local or national government and I'm always astounded by the variety of opinions, especially over important matters of process. It's especially true when bodies have been merged together and even years later you see the differences in attitude. I've witnessed really heated debates over policy on things like the level of leniency managers use over Christmas holidays. Although the rule book said one thing, there were people in the room who had made their own ruling and were living by it. I'm not particularly advocating this, as in the end you could have anarchy, but it does go to show that there is some flex in the system'.

Find the time

Common problems are things like too much time spent in meetings, a daily deluge of email to deal with, unreasonable workloads and conflicting demands from above. Some of the potential consequences, which also have to be dealt with include workplace disputes between colleagues, or over process issues and operational matters. The ensuing stress this can cause may lead to sickness absence eating up more of our valuable time.

Even if you make only a marginal improvement, you will enhance and enrich your own working life or that of your colleagues, which should act as an incentive to continue to change. If you opt for this route, ensure the alterations you make are in line with the core purpose of the organisation. If you work in retail and decide to stop attending certain meetings, make sure the time you spend is devoted to doing something which enhances the customer experience, in this way, your decision is inarguable.

For all the books written on time management, laden with tools and tips, the most significant point to remember is 'you have more control over your time than you often realise'. Deciding the nature and order of tasks each day makes you realise just how much flexibility there is. Even if you are a 'detail person' it is worth reminding yourself now and again that not everything you do needs to be gold plated.

Retain perspective

We encounter countless examples through our lives of 'perspective change'. A problem which seems immense in the middle of the night, is somehow lessened in the light of day. If we feel unwell, we vow to value every moment as soon as we get better. A major event can trigger a desire to 'live life to the full'.

So perspective is good for shaping a more realistic view of the world, and keeping our issues in their rightful place. This can form an excellent backdrop to changing our behaviours in pursuit of wellbeing. If we can realistically assess what is going on in the workplace, we may not need to change things as much as we first thought.

It is hard to remind ourselves each day of how lucky we are, to be fit and healthy, have good friends and faithful family, a roof over our heads and food to eat. The pressures on us, from what is thought to be societal norms, mean we often go chasing the dream by working harder and longer.

The difficulty with this is we cannot measure our happiness by comparing ourselves to others, only by deciding what matters to us. If a bigger house, flashier car, more expensive holiday looks like a goal worth chasing, we normally find our comfort level increases, but we are not necessarily happier.

The minute we begin to set our own agenda on wellbeing, we free ourselves from the money trap.

Maintain resilience

Linked to perspective is resilience, one of the foundation stones of wellbeing, if we can 'keep our head when all around are losing theirs', we've got the problem cracked.

Like 'perspective', a large part of resilience is being able to take the long view, and see things for what they really are. Sometimes, when we have a problem, we need to sleep on it, and if we know things will look better tomorrow, we are better able to cope today.

Our resilience builds if we take an attitude which is realistic. Knowing things will sometimes go wrong, helps us to cope when they do, and this type of stoicism engenders confidence in those around us.

We can learn too from the modern approach to treating depression, where 'talking therapies' are used. One of the underpinning principles of these methods is the knowledge that though there are many things we can't change, what we can do is alter our view of them. Once we have been 'enabled' with this power, the difficulties we face may feel significantly reduced.

Infect someone

We should never underestimate our ability to change other people's outlook and mood by the way we behave when we're with them.

Contrast the following two stories about managers

Paula

'I work in a small team with the moodiest manager I have ever come across. Because of what I do, I am away from my desk for large parts of the day, either at meetings or seeing clients. My 3 colleagues aren't so lucky.

You can feel the tension in the morning as we wait for the boss to appear. What kind of mood she is in affects the whole team and if the day gets off to a bad start we know it's downhill all the way.

I feel really sorry for the others because they have no escape. The bad moods are only a part of the problem. Sometimes it's the not knowing which gets to everyone'.

Janette

'Inspirational, that's the word I'd use to describe my first manager. She just had this way about her, the minute she entered the room you knew everything was going to be alright. Even if we'd been struggling to hit deadlines or tackling some awful problem, it was her passion and enthusiasm which translated itself to the whole team. What's more, she always had a smile on her face, it made us all feel happier.'

We have seen the 'infectious' nature of stress, how it can translate itself from one person to the next. At the other end of the mood scale, we've all had the sensation of infectious laughter, we simply cannot stop ourselves from following the herd.

So, if we have the opportunity to set the mood for people around us each day, shouldn't we treat that with a degree of responsibility, and do our level best to make sure we are positive?

Get your mood right, keep your stress under control and the calmness will spread.

Conclusions

There is nothing to stop you taking action, little will happen if you don't

Empowerment is illusory, just do it and see what happens

Keep your perspective and resilience will follow

How you are is how those close to you are – infect them

CHAPTER 21

A.O.B.

In this final chapter, we wrap up with some thoughts on where you could begin to make a difference, they are more 'idea catalysts' than proscriptive behaviours, just a starting point for your own thinking.

We also take a final look at where the future may lie for you personally, with regard to your decisions about happiness, well-being and commitment to the cause.

Ten ideas for starters

1. Declare your workspace a clutter-free zone. Give yourself a target of an hour to put everything you 'own' into a box, all the paraphernalia in and around your desk or working area. Only put back that which you use on a daily basis. From what is left in the box, allow yourself three additional useful items. Store everything else somewhere for a month – after that if it hasn't been used, ditch it.

2. Set up a sporting challenge at work. Get a few likely suspects together (the ones who look fit already), and brainstorm ideas. A squash league, netball team or swimming club would all work. Agree some rules and goals, like the frequency you will participate and what you hope to achieve.

3. Get everyone in your team to write a 50 word piece outlining something good they did for another person in the

last month. Don't be limited by work-based activity and avoid being judgemental. Stick them up and create a 'wall of giving', leave it up for a month so that others can read the stories.

4. Have a quarterly draw for a day off. Agree with the team that whoever gets lucky, you will help them by picking up their workload for that day, so they're not faced with a backlog when they return. Suggest that winners' names don't go into the next draw, so others have a better chance.

5. Write down your top ten values in life, the things you would not like to be without (family, friends, integrity, inclusion etc.), now pick the top 5 and try to make sure you live up to them for the next month.

6. Volunteer. Read up in the local paper or research online to find a nearby project which needs a helping hand. Spend time running a community centre, do some unpaid work in a charity shop, help local old folks by doing their shopping.

7. Make one Friday a 'feelings' day. Express as openly and honestly as you can how you feel about those close to you, in work, at home or as part of your wider circle of contacts.

8. Over the course of a month, write 12 letters. They can be to anyone about anything, a thank you note, a catch up with an old friend, a missive to your mother. Deciding who to send them to is part of the enjoyment, after that the content will write itself.

9. Treat yourself to an hour off. Don't let other distractions get in the way, go for a walk and try to appreciate what's around you. If you don't manage this four times a year (once for each season) you are working too hard.

10. Pass comment. Strike up a conversation at the supermarket checkout, while waiting for a bus or walking the dog. Chat to people in work who aren't in your department and find out what they do.

End notes on happiness and wellbeing

The future you

Fast forward through your life, and imagine what it is going to be like when you look back. If you use this technique to visualise different outcomes, it may change the way you live your life now.

Many people try to counsel and advise us through our lives. We have all heard parents or grandparents telling us to appreciate our youth as it's so quickly gone, and it is true that the journey is a short one. For the most part we want to make sure we get the very best out of it, so time spent worrying about money or situations we cannot change is a waste.

Instead it is better to pledge an existence of 'no regrets', so we're not faced with a litany of lost opportunities which we rue in retrospect.

It is most likely happiness is a combination of nature and nurture, a theme we considered right at the start of this book. There is little point fretting over how much of the happiness gene we inherited, as we can now do little to influence it. Isn't it more important to consider, within the confines of our hereditary happiness, how we can maximise our potential for feeling good?

It is here where wellbeing behaviours can play their part. By doing the right things regularly and relentlessly, the studies show we can increase our chances of being happier.

Selfish or selfless

By nature we tend to be selfish beings, perhaps because we each have an instinct based on 'survival of the fittest'. Society, culture and media have a role here too. Those who lived through the 1980s will remember it was the era of the 'me-society.' It was perhaps best epitomised in the film *Wall Street*, where the central character, a hard and ruthless financier, Gordon Gecko, proclaims, (and this is paraphrased) 'Greed is good!'. We are encouraged to 'look after number one'.

At the other end of the spectrum is the 'virtuous' person; someone who will put themselves out for others, who is considerate and selfless. It is often hard to see where their reward comes from, certainly the likes of Gecko would find them difficult to comprehend.

Are these two states incompatible? We suggest not and furthermore would advance the theory they are both a part of wellbeing and happiness. If we buy into the idea that we can infect other people with our mood, we have a duty to make sure this is a positive experience. It's much better to infect someone with happiness than angst. So the starting point must be our own wellbeing, only then, when we are 'at one' can we let ourselves loose on a wider circle of people.

So the pursuit of our own happiness can be seen in terms of an initial selfishness, with wider, grander motives of selflessness behind it. If it is also true our self-worth, peace of mind and wellbeing are fuelled by making someone else's world better, giving of ourselves is an act which benefits both parties. Give a homeless person some change and they will get to eat that day, increasing their wellbeing. At the same time, knowing we have made someone else's life better enriches us.

Experiential happiness

Beside the behaviours we have outlined, is there anything else we could do which would make us happier? The answer is simple, we just need to consider the experiences which have given us pleasure in the past and do more of them. This may sound a little facile, but often we allow other things in our lives to get in the way.

Alfie

'I'm suffering from what I've named "we must do this again soon" syndrome. It was 12 years after Uni that a bunch of us got together for a few beers and a lot of laughs. As with all great friendships, we slipped back into it like we'd never been apart.

It wasn't just the beer talking when I said "we must do this again soon", I really meant it, these guys had once meant the world to me, they'd picked me up when I was down, lent me money when I was short, supported me in so many practical and emotional ways and I'd tried to do the same for them when the occasion arose. I realised that nothing had changed, we had a shared history and they still meant the world to me.

That was 8 years ago and I haven't seen them since.

I have no idea why, but I suspect it's my fault!'

Expectation happiness

With a sunny demeanour, a bright outlook and a personal attitude which says 'nothing can possibly go wrong' we take control and set our own agenda for happiness. Anticipation of the best in everything is much more likely to produce a positive result than the feeling the world is about to crumble.

This may be nothing more than a 'glass half full' way of looking at the world, but the physical and wellbeing effects of a positive psyche can be very real indeed. A great example of this is shown by our sense of taste. For many years, manufacturers have conducted 'blind tastings' with groups of potential consumers. One such study presented whisky drinkers with six unlabelled bottles only one of which had the distinctive triangular shape of a well known premium brand. The majority of respondents placed this whisky at the top of their list, using words to describe it such as smooth and mellow, in fact exactly the terms which distillers use on their labels, to infer quality.

The truth is there was no difference between the whiskies, each bottle's contents were identical.

As in so many situations, it is not the reality of what is happening which governs our resilience, our pleasure or our angst, it is the interpretation we place upon it. Knowing this is not enough to force ourselves happy, but it is a key part of the 'perceptual happiness' used in talking therapies, which we discussed in the preceding chapter.

Taste and fashion go hand-in-hand, not just in clothes, but also in home décor and even what we eat and drink. Sweet German wines were all the rage in the seventies, when few people in the U.K. were familiar with wine drinking, over time, tastes switched to drier wines, now the pendulum has swung back some. The wines haven't changed, but how we think and talk about them and the effect they have on us has.

Hedonistic frustration

The principles of wellbeing and happiness are better understood now than at any other time. Some of the things which may have felt instinctively right in the past, such as 'reach out and be kind to others' have been researched and validated, but there is still a note of caution to sound about the pursuit of happiness.

Valid though it is that we may want to live the most enriched lives possible and in equal measure it is true that the behaviours we talk about will contribute positively to this, it is also thought if we chase happiness for it's own sake, we may become so wrapped up in trying to locate it, we may actually prevent it.

It is thought much more likely that if we pursue other things, good things, right things, we will find contentment as a consequence.

Knowing this may enable us to double bluff ourselves. If we create the right environment for wellbeing, encourage people to harmonise their working and leisure lives and adopt the well-researched behavioural pattern which promotes a greater sense of oneness, we should find our lives are enriched as a consequence. Stopping to think about this occasionally, raising our consciousness of our wellbeing quest will not burst the bubble, but becoming fixated by it may.

And finally…

There is great news about wellbeing. It is on the agenda. A generation ago, people in work were either well or not, and if it were the latter, the organisation would deal with it in one of a number of unsympathetic ways. People would be 'managed out', the problem would be ignored or they would be given less and less fulfilling tasks. Being unwell in the workplace was seen as a sign of weakness, certainly not a trait of good future leaders.

Because of this, many were forced to stay silent, some still do, but the picture is changing and forward-thinking organisations are beginning to engage with the necessity to keep their people well, not just physically.

The reasons they do this almost don't matter, but our chapter covering the 3 cases for change provides a rationale across scientific, organisational and emotional factors. We've said it before, happy workers are productive workers, if organisations are motivated by self-interest rather than altruism, so be it, the outcome is that they are paying more attention to wellbeing.

As individuals we can play our part too. If we accept we have a genetic disposition to 'happiness' then we have a duty of care *to ourselves* to maximise our potential by 'living well'. This is not advocacy of a hair-shirt mentality, it is about balance. Underpin your behaviour with the right things, but don't forget to give yourself a day off now and again, it's not a police state for happiness, just a set of suggestions.

Blend your own outlook and behaviours into the workplace, and the individuals around you will begin to be infected, eventually everyone will be doing the right thing and the world of commerce will be healed of all its ills.

Utopia is just around the corner; don't forget to take a packed lunch for the journey.

Ashforth, B. (1994) 'Petty Tyranny in Organizations'. *Human Relations*, 47(7): 755–78.

Bass, B. (1997) *Transformational Leadership*. New Jersey: Lawrence Erlbaum.

Bowles, D. and Cooper, C. L. (2009) *Employee Morale*. London: Palgrave Macmillan.

Cooper, C. L. et al (2009) *Environment on Mental Wellbeing: Mental Capital and Wellbeing*. Oxford: Wiley-Blackwell.

Cooper, C. L. and Dewe, P. (2008) 'Wellbeing, Absenteeism & Presenteeism: Costs and Challenges'. *Occupational Medicine*, 58(8): 552–4.

Cooper, R., Boyko, C. and Codinhoto, R. (2009) 'The Effect of the Physical Environment on Mental Wellbeing', in Cooper, C. L. et al (2009): *Mental Capital & Wellbeing*. Oxford: Wiley-Blackwell.

Covey, S. (2004) *The 7 Habits of Highly Effective People*. New York: Simon & Schuster.

Cropanzano, R. and Wright, T. M. (2007) *The Happy/Productive Worker Thesis Revisited*. 'Research in Personnel and Human Resources Management' (Vol. 26) Elsevier.

Dixon, S. (2003) *Implications of Population Ageing for the Labour Market*. Labour Market Trends, February, pp. 67–76. London: Office for National Statistics.

Dolan, P., Layard, R. and Metcalfe, R. (2011) *Measuring Subjective Wellbeing for Public Policy*. London: ONS.

Donald, I. et al (2005) 'The Experience of Work-related Stress Across Occupations'. *Journal of Managerial Psychology*, 20(2): 170–87.

DTI (2006) *How Have Employees Fared: Recent UK Trends. Employment Relations Research Series No. 56*. London: Department of Trade and Industry.

Finkelstein, S. and Cooper, C. L. (2010) *Advances in Mergers & Acquisitions*. Bingley: Emerald Publ.

Goleman, D. (1996) *Emotional Intelligence: Why It Can Matter More Than IQ*. London: Bloomsbury Publishing PLC.

Hemp, P. (2004) 'Presenteeism: At Work—But Out Of It'. *Harvard Business Review*, October 2004, pp. 49–58.

Hosie, P. and Cooper, C. L. (2006) *Happy Performing Manager*. Cheltenham: Edward Elgar Publ.

Isles, N. (2005) *The Joy of Work?* London: The Work Foundation.

Karasek, R. et al (1998) 'The Job Centred Questionnaire'. *Journal of Occupational Health Psychology*, 3(4): 322–55.

Lewis, S. and Cooper, C. L. (2005) *Work-Life Integration*. Chichester: Wiley & Sons.

177

Luft, J. and Ingham, H. (1955) 'The Johari Window: A Graphic Model of Interpersonal Awareness'. Proceedings of the western training laboratory in group development. Los Angeles: UCLA.

Lundberg, U. and Cooper, C. L. (2010) *The Science of Occupational Health*. Oxford: Wiley-Blackwell.

Maslow, A. (1954) *Motivation and Personality*. NY: Harper & Row.

McDonald, N. (1989) 'Jobs and Their Environment: The Psychological Impact of Work in Noise'. *The Irish Journal of Psychology*, 10: 33–50.

McGregor, D. (1960) *The Human Side of Enterprise*. New York: McGraw-Hill.

Oswald, A. (1997) 'Happiness and Economic Performance'. *Economic Journal*, 107: 1815–31.

Oswald, A. and Wu, S. (2009) 'Objective Confirmation of Subjective Measures of Human Well-being'. *Science*, 27: 576–9.

Rayner, C., Hoel, H. and Cooper, C. L. (2002) *Workplace Bullying*. London: Taylor & Francis.

Robertson, I. and Flint-Taylor, J. (2009) 'Leadership, Psychology Well-being and Organizational Outcomes', in Cartwright, S. and Cooper, C. L. *Oxford Handbook of Organizational Well-being*. Oxford: Oxford University Press.

Robertson, I. and Cooper, C. L. (2011) *Wellbeing: Happiness and Productivity at Work*. London: Palgrave Macmillan.

Seligman, M. (2002) *Authentic Happiness*. NY: Free Press.

Smeaton, B., Young, V. and Spencer, S. (2007) 'The Future of Work: Employers and Workplace Transformation'. Working Paper Series No. 56. Manchester: Equal Opportunities Commission.

Sundstrom, E. (1986) *Workplaces: The Psychology of the Physical Environment in Offices and Factories*. New York: Cambridge University.

Swan, J. and Cooper, C. L. (2005) *Time, Health and the Family*. London: Working Families.

Tepper, B. J. (2000) 'Consequences of Abusive Supervision'. *Academy of Management Journal*, 43: 178–90.

Van Dierendonck, D., Haynes, C., Borrit, C. and Stride, C. (2004) 'Leadership Behaviour and Subordinate Wellbeing'. *Journal of Occupational Health Psychology*, 9: 165–75.

Further Reading

Albrecht, S. (2010) *Handbook of Employee Engagement*. Cheltenham: Edward Elgar Publ.

Allvin, M. et al (2011) *Work Without Boundaries: Psychological Perspectives on the New Working Life*. Oxford: Wiley-Blackwell.

Bowles, D. and Cooper, C. L (2009) *Employee Morale: Driving Performance in Challenging Times*. London: Palgrave Macmillan.

Cartwright, S. and Cooper, C. L. (2009) *The Oxford Handbook of Organizational Wellbeing*. Oxford: Oxford University Press.

Greenfield, S., McGregory (1960) *The Human Side of Enterprise*. New York: McGraw Hill.

Kinder, A., Hughes, R. and Cooper, C. L. (2008) *Employee Wellbeing Support: A Workplace Resource*. Oxford: Wiley-Blackwell.

Layard, R. (2005) *Happiness: Lessons from a New Science*. London: Penguin Books.

Passmore, J. (2010) *Excellence in Coaching*. London: Kogan Page.

Powdthavee, N. (2010) *The Happiness Equation*. London: Icon Books.

Quick, J. et al (2008) *Managing Executive Health: Personal and Corporate Strategies for Sustained Success*. Cambridge: Cambridge University Press.

Weinberg, A. et al (2010) *Organizational Stress Management*. London: Palgrave Macmillan.